Juan Timonin
September, 1996

Interpreting Scripture in the Third Millennium

Walter Vogels

Interpreting Scripture in the Third Millennium

Author – Reader – Text

NOVALIS

Biblical quotations are from *The Jerusalem Bible.*

Cover and layout: Gilles Lépine

Business Office: Novalis, P.O. Box 990,
Outremont, Quebec H2V 4S7 Canada

ISBN 2 89088-613-1

Printed in Canada

Canadian Cataloguing in Publication Data

Vogels, Walter, 1932-
Interpreting Scripture in the third millenium:
author, reader, text

(Novalis theological series)
Includes bibliographical references.
ISBN 2-89088-613-1

1. Bible—Criticism, interpretation, etc.
2. Bible—Hermeneutics. I. Title. II. Series.

BS476.V64 1993 220.6 C93-090260-2

NOVALIS

Table of Contents

II: The Reader Gives Meaning

III: The Text Is the Judge

Foreword

The three chapters of this book present in slightly revised form the three public lectures I delivered as the *Elizabeth Seton Lectures* at Mount Saint Vincent University in Halifax, Nova Scotia, on October 6-7, 1992.

The purpose of these lectures, held every year at the University through its Department of Religious Studies, is to bring to the campus "outstanding expressions of Christian thought and life… [to] help us all to bring our minds and hearts to bear upon the challenge of the time."

One of the major challenges in biblical studies in our time is how we should approach the Bible. Our time, more than any other, is witness to an explosion of different methods of biblical interpretation. This explosion has caused misunderstandings and even conflicts between the scholars belonging to the different schools. For students and Bible readers, this explosion of methods has created confusion and sometimes discouragement from all scientific study of the Bible. And still, the respect we owe to the Word of God demands that we approach the Bible with the best tools available, because we can only be inspired by and live according to the Bible if we really understand it. A simplistic, naive reading of the Bible will rarely achieve that transformation of our lives.

The confusion that exists about reading in general is well described by Edwin M. Good:

> For those who read for a reason other than to give rein to fantasy or to amass mere facts, however, reading has disintegrated. We have become uncertain about what a text is and about why we read. According to the semioticians, a text is a congeries of codes to be cracked. To the structuralists, it is a system of signifiers. The deconstructionists tell us that a text has already undermined itself and means a whole host of contraries. The hermeneuts are sure that a text is (1) something that means or (2) that properly means only what its author meant or (3) that probably never means what its author meant. The reception theorists tell us that it means what *we* think it means. The psychoanalytic critics deny this, on the grounds that we do not know what we think. The political critics have decided that a text means what "they" think it means, because a text is always a product of those in power. Historical critics may insist that the text means only what it used to mean.[1]

The purpose of the lectures, and thus of this book, is to guide the reader through this forest of biblical methods. No one method is perfect, no one can do everything, but each one has its advantages as well as its limitations.

I dedicate this book to the Department of Religious Studies at Mount Saint Vincent University and, in a special way, to Professor Jacques Goulet, head of the Department, in gratitude for the honour of having been invited to present the *Elizabeth Seton Lectures*.

Walter Vogels

---

[1] E. M. Good, *In Turns of Tempest: A Reading of Job* (Stanford, California: Stanford University Press, 1990), p. 177.

Introduction

Humans are social beings. We communicate with each other in many different ways. We use conventional signs, we paint, we play music, but above all we speak to each other and we write. The spoken and the written word are the most common ways of communicating. Communication presupposes two persons: someone, the sender, who tries to express him- or herself and another person, the receiver. This person is not a tape-recorder who registers what is expressed but is a living person who necessarily interprets what is seen, heard or read. Any teacher knows that students do not all understand the same thing! We may hear or read the same words, but we understand them differently.

The Bible being a written text does not escape this principle. If people read the Bible, they interpret the Bible, and this, as we all know, is indeed what has happened over the centuries. The Bible has been read and interpreted in many different ways. Since we too read the Bible, it is perhaps useful to reflect on what we are doing, how we are doing it, what we are looking for, and from what perspective we interpret.

We spoke of the sender and the receiver in human communication, but in any written communication there is also the text itself. Three actors are thus involved in the Bible: the author, the text and the reader. Until very recently all attention went to the author, but presently the two forgotten actors have received more attention in biblical studies. We can even speak of three types of interpretation according to which of the three actors is favoured. An author-centred interpretation looks for the world behind the text, a text-centred interpretation looks for the world within the text, and a reader-centred interpretation looks for the world in front of the text. Each one has its advantages but also its limitations. These different approaches may lead to different results and thus several questions arise, for instance, Who decides upon the 'real' or 'true' meaning of the text? How do these three types of interpretation relate to each other? Where is biblical studies heading? Which approach will be preferred in the third millennium?

Each of the three chapters will look at one of these three types of interpretation. Each chapter will explain the presuppositions and the theory of the chosen interpretation and then show how this affects the reading of a text. The text I have chosen as test case is the paradise story in Genesis (2:4b–3:24) because everybody in our culture has heard about the garden of Eden, Adam and Eve, the rib, the apple and the serpent.[1] This story is well known, but is it ever interpreted in different ways! What is the relation of this story to the world?[2] Does it describe what once was — historical events? What is now — our world? What will be — vision? What should be — ideal or utopia? What isn't — irony? We will conclude each chapter with a short reflection on the advantages and limitations of the approach taken.

[1] W. Vogels, *Bijbellezen Nu* (Mechelen: Werkgenootschap voor Catechese, 1982).

[2] P. D. Miscall, "Jacques Derrida in the Garden of Eden," in *Union Seminary Quarterly Review,* 44 (1990), pp. 1-9; Y. Amit, "Biblical Utopianism: A Mapmakers Guide to Eden," in *Union Seminary Quarterly Review,* 44 (1990), pp. 11-17.

I

The Intention of the Author

I. Presuppositions and Theory of an Author-centred Interpretation

The most obvious thing we can say about a text is that someone wrote it. There would be no book without the writer, whom we may suspect of having written the text because he or she wanted to communicate something. A writer wants to be read and thus certainly intended to write a meaningful text. It appears then that the right thing to do for the reader is to try to discover what the author intended to say. The Bible may be inspired, but it was still written by humans. When in the liturgy we proclaim the gospel, we start by saying: "A reading from the holy gospel according to Matthew" and we conclude by saying: "The word of God." The Bible is indeed word of God, but no less word of humans. Not surprising then that people, after one has given the exegesis of a text, may ask: "Do you really think that this is what Matthew wanted to say? Do you believe that the writer was thinking of all that?" People search for the intention of the biblical writer.

If you happen to be a writer, you certainly will agree that readers should try to respect what you want to say. Nothing is more frustrating than to read a review of a book you have written in which the reviewer has clearly missed the point. You are upset and wish that the reviewer had read the book more carefully. We even speak of the rights of the author!

The importance of the writer is often evident in the reasons people give for buying a particular book. They may like the style or the insights of a particular author and buy any new book published by that person. Were Mitchener to write another novel or Schillebeeckx another theological study, we may be certain that these books would sell thousands of copies. If archaeologists were to discover an old document somewhere in Israel, it would immediately attract the attention of scholars, but can you image the excitement if that document were proved to have been written by Paul!

When I read a letter from my best friend, I certainly will try to find out what she wanted to tell me. Because we are so close to each other and because such letters are written in a familiar language, I may hope to succeed quite well, even if experience tells us that we sometimes misinterpret even then. But this is a very unique type of written communication. The degree of difficulty involved in interpreting a written text depends on two basic variables, one related to who wrote and the other to what and how that person wrote.

The first variable is the degree to which the writer and the reader share a common world of discourse and experience. This degree is optimal between two friends belonging to the same culture, but may already become more complicated if they belong to two different language groups, and the problem can become extremely complicated if writer and reader belong to totally different periods in time, different cultures, have never seen each other and do not know each other. The difficulty in discovering the intention of the writer increases even further if the reader is not the reader addressed by the writer, for instance, if another person reads the letter I received from my friend.

The second variable is the degree to which the text involves specialized content and form of expression. Friends easily understand the love letters they write to each other, but it becomes more difficult to understand letters using technical language and forms, such as letters written by notaries or lawyers.

Everybody realizes that for the reading of the Bible we are not at all in the optimal conditions, but on the contrary in the most difficult, because of the distance in time and space between the writer and the reader, who is no longer even the originally intended reader. Paul wrote a letter to the Romans of his day and not to us here in Canada approaching the third millennium. Also, some of the forms used in the Bible may cause special problems.

The letters of Paul are not exactly written in easy language and the Book of Revelation is very mysterious to the modern reader.

An author-centred interpretation of the Bible has thus an important but difficult task to discover the intention of the writer. The whole world behind the text, which includes the cultural, the ideological, the historical, the linguistic, the social and the political conditions in which the writer was living, has to be uncovered. This is obvious if the author has a precise event in mind, but even if he or she is writing about a more universal truth, even then the person remains within a particular context. The knowledge of these circumstances can give a very new understanding of the text. This principle was clearly affirmed by Vatican II:

> The interpreter must investigate what meaning the sacred writer intended to express and actually expressed in particular circumstances as he used contemporary literary forms in accordance with the situation of his own time and culture (*Dogmatic Constitution on Divine Revelation,* § 12).

A few examples taken from profane literature may illustrate this. Any reader can understand what Dante writes about some cardinals in his *Divine Comedy*. But it adds a new dimension to the text if one knows that these cardinals were not pure literary fictions, but real historical people of his time.

Marcel Proust started writing his famous book *A la recherche du temps perdu* in 1909, changed it continually and finished it in 1922 just before he died. One could read this book and enjoy it without knowing anything about the author, as Proust himself admits. The 'I' in the book, the narrator, speaks of his great love for a young woman, Albertine Simonet. But after reading Proust's biography, one understands the book quite differently. The 'I,' the narrator, is in fact Proust, a homosexual, and Albertine, the woman in the story, is in fact a man, Albert, Proust's secretary and driver who lived with Proust, separated and finally was killed in a plane crash.

Let us now look at some of the different contexts belonging to the world of the writer and how they influence the understanding of the text.

1. The Geographical Context

A writer always lives somewhere. When we speak to a person from a different part of the world, the relationship with that person changes totally if we happen to have visited that place. The fact that we know the geographical context of that person may even create a special link. Any person who has had the opportunity to visit Israel and has seen Mount Sinai, Jerusalem and the Lake of Galilee, has noticed how some biblical texts speak in a new way.

The paradise story contains several references to geography. The garden is placed "in Eden which is in the east" (Gen 2:8). "The east," for people living in Israel, was of course the region of Mesopotamia, the region of the great cultures. We have no information about where to locate "Eden," but the stem of the word could point to the meaning of 'pleasure.' Would we then have something like Disneyland in California or Disneyworld in Florida? The text mentions four rivers and the places where those rivers flow (2:10-14). While the details remain unclear, at least two of the rivers, the Tigris and the Euphrates, are well known as the two great rivers of Mesopotamia. There is obviously a lot of water in that paradise. Anyone who has seen these two great rivers will read the text differently, and anyone who has visited Israel will be aware of the importance of water: what a struggle for the farmers there in that dry climate. In the garden, at least, there was water in abundance, not to mention the gold, the bdellium and onyx stone also found there (2:12). It was indeed a real paradise!

2. The Historical Context

A writer and his or her readers also live in a particular period in time. To understand some of the present constitutional problems in Canada, we have to know something of Canada's history. It is always interesting to read a newspaper from several years ago and to learn what people paid then for food or for houses. Similarly, it would help the reader to discover in what historical context the paradise story was written. As we will see later, some scholars believe that it was written at the time of Solomon, the only period in Israel's history when it was a world empire, a time of great prosperity, a time that could be compared to a paradise. Some scholars believe that the preceding text, the creation narrative (1:1–2:4a), was written at the time of the exile, a time of despair, misery and chaos. It is, therefore, not surprising that an author living at the time of Israel's greatest misery writes differently from an author writing at the time of Israel's greatest prosperity.

3. The Cultural Context

All people have their own culture. After I had explained something to a student from Sri Lanka, I asked him if he had understood. I was expecting him to nod his head, up-down, like we do to say 'yes,' but instead he moved his head from left to right, which I interpreted as a 'no.' So I repeated my explanation and my question and got the same result. Only then did I realize that the sign language of the two cultures is different. How many misunderstandings there are because of different cultural signs!

The serpent plays an important role in the paradise story, but what is the connotation it evokes for the reader? The text says very clearly that the serpent is an animal, and not satan as many people are inclined to believe. It "was the most subtle of all the wild beasts that Yahweh God had made" (3:1). But how we feel today about serpents may be very different from how people felt about them in biblical times. Archaeologists have discovered small statues of a naked goddess with a serpent round her breasts, which shows that for the author and the original readers the serpent was connected with the cult of Baal and Astarte, a fertility cult. Serpents had something to do with the mystery of life and death. Not too many modern readers would spontaneously think in those terms, even if we still consider the serpent the symbol of medicine.

4. The Social and the Political Context

The social and political conditions in which a writer lives will also affect his or her writings. The paradise story speaks in many places about the relationship between husband and wife. “Your yearning shall be for your husband, yet he will lord it over you” (3:16). The last part of this sentence is lived differently in the great variety of societies in the world, and even in the same society this may have changed over the centuries. The accursed soil will be worked “with sweat on your brow” (3:18-19). This also is very different in various parts of the world, according to the soil, the tools and the climate.

5. The Linguistic Context

We have mentioned several contexts, but another very important one is the linguistic context, because after all we are speaking of a written text. This has again special implications for the understanding of the biblical text.

a. Language

When we say ‘text,’ we know that this implies that it is written in a particular language. The language of the greatest part of the Bible is Hebrew (Greek for the New Testament). Each language has its own characteristics, its own richness and its own limitations. Any person who has ever translated a text knows what that means. For example, the English language has three pronouns it can use for a third person singular subject: ‘he,’ ‘she,’ and ‘it,’ but the French language has only two: ‘il’ and ‘elle.’

So the French 'il' becomes in an English translation 'he' or 'it.' The Hebrew language too has only two pronouns, 'hu' and 'hi,' and therefore 'hu' can refer to the masculine 'he' or the neutral 'it.' This, as we will see, has consequences when it comes to the understanding of a very much disputed passage of the paradise story (3:15).

b. Words

Each language uses words, but words do not always and everywhere have the same connotation. When we in Canada speak of 'winter,' we know what that means: snow, ice, cold, boots, warm clothes; we may even think of evenings round the fireplace or of Christmas. In Australia, where people speak the same English language, they also use the word 'winter.' But winter, according to the different regions there, may correspond to temperatures of 20 to 30° Celsius and has nothing to do with snow and cold and certainly nothing to do with Christmas, because Australians have winter in July and August when we have summer. Thus, it is important when we read an English text to know if the author was Australian or Canadian.

The dating of a text also has implications for understanding. If I read the word 'gay' in a text written by a Canadian author, it is important to know *when* this text was written because the meaning of that word has changed over the years.

In the paradise story there are several references to nakedness, "Now both of them were naked, the man and his wife, but they felt no shame in front of each other"

(2:25; 3:7, 10, 11). In our culture nakedness and nudity often have sexual connotations; people may think of a striptease, of *Playboy,* or whatever. The word in the biblical tradition evokes a very different concept, similar to what it sometimes does for us. When we say, "I am naked in front of you," we mean that we are totally honest, without any masks, that we appear as we are. Nakedness refers to our limitations and our vulnerability. Man and woman in paradise are not ashamed of what they are, they accept themselves and each other as they are.

c. Sentence

But words are used in sentences, and suddenly something interesting happens. It may well be that I understand all the words, but have no idea what the sentence really means. There is the beautiful song by Crystal Gail, *Don't You Make My Brown Eyes Blue.* To understand that statement, one has to know that in English 'blue' is not necessarily 'blue,' even if 'brown' is 'brown.' Only a person who knows the language very well notices that the isotopy changes in the sentence, moving from colour to a state of mind.

We probably understand all the words of the following sentence of the paradise story: "This is why a man leaves his father and mother and joins himself to his wife, and they become one body" (2:24). But how can two become literally "one body"? Since people often connect the nakedness of the following verse (2:25) with sex, they then assume that becoming "one body" refers to sexual intercourse for procreation. The sentence, however, has a much deeper meaning. It refers to the change from a son's loyalty to his parents to a man's loyalty to his wife. They become a new unit, indeed a new body. Similarly, Christians speak of the mystical body of Christ.

d. Literary Genre

Many different sentences make up a literary unit and each unit has its own literary genre. We never can stress enough the importance of this. Inability or unwillingness to adjust to the literary genre leads of course to the worst misunderstandings. When I am telling my students a joke and they think I am serious, that is their problem. But if I am serious and they think I am joking, they are in trouble. Readers generally adjust automatically to the literary genre of a text. When a text begins, "Once upon a time,..." everyone knows that this text is a fairytale.

After David had committed adultery with Bathsheba and had murdered Uriah her husband (2 Samuel 11), the prophet Nathan came to David and said to him: "In the same town were two men, one rich, the other poor. The rich man had flocks and herds in great abundance; the poor man had nothing but a ewe lamb, one only, a small one he had bought... When there came a traveller to stay, the rich man refused to take one of his own flock or herd to provide for the wayfarer who had come to him. Instead he took the poor man's lamb and prepared it for his guest." David, furious that such a thing could happen in Jerusalem, the city where he as king was responsible for justice, declared "the man who did this deserves to die." To which the prophet Nathan replied: "You are the man" (2 Sam 12:1-7). This is a clear example of misunderstanding about the literary genre of what was said. David, not realizing that Nathan was telling a parable, understood the story as a historical report of something that happened in Jerusalem. This misunderstanding resulted in David determining his own penalty.

What seems so obvious for all texts becomes a problem and even a topic of endless discussion for many people when it comes to the reading of the Bible. The paradise story, like any other text, must have its own literary genre. Any intelligent reader who reads a story in which an animal speaks knows that the text is not factual, but belongs to a type of literature in which the imagination plays a large role. And speak is precisely what the serpent, one of "the wild beasts that Yahweh God had made," does: "It asked the woman" (Gen 3:1). Real serpents do not speak; they can speak only in fairytales.

In nature or in botanical gardens, one does not find a "tree of life" or a "tree of the knowledge of good and evil" (2:9). The story obviously cannot be a historical report of events from the beginning of the world because nobody has information about what happened thousands, perhaps millions, of years ago, before the dawn of recorded history.

People all over the world have reflected upon the deep truths about God, about humanity, its nature and origin, about suffering, death, work, love, and also about the world around us, and have expressed this in what are called 'myths.' Myth must be understood in the modern sense of the word, as an attempt to express in symbolic story form a transcendental reality or truth grasped intuitively. So even if it did not happen exactly as described in the myth, the myth speaks of truth and reality. The variety of myths all over the world is the best proof that humans have grasped something of the realities of the mysteries of life, although it may be in different ways. Since reality can never be adequately comprehended, myth admits that more than one approach can be valid.

Another way to determine the literary genre of a text such as the paradise story is to speak of a prophecy of the past. Prophets are people who are concerned primarily with the present, but who, by looking at the present, can say something about the future, about where people's behaviour will lead them. By looking at the present, they also can say important things about the past. For example, when we look at the waters of Canada's Great Lakes, we know that in some years from now they will be hopelessly polluted unless something is done *now*, but we can also deduce that these waters must have been pure years ago. The writer of the paradise story, by looking at how people lived in his day, could certainly say very valuable and true things about the ideal world that he projected into the past like other biblical writers and, like we all do, hope for an ideal world in the future.

Even if a first superficial reading of the paradise story leaves the impression that the text describes a precise geographic, and thus historical, place for the garden of Eden, our ignorance of the location of Eden and of two of the rivers, Pishon and Gihon, confirms that these details are included simply to place the myth on earth in an ideal world. The writer speaks of four rivers because the symbolic number four represents the four corners of the world: the water of the whole world was there, and even gold and precious stones. This was indeed paradise!

e. Book

Many literary units together form a book. The composition of a book can be very simple, as when an author writes chapter after chapter, then publishes the product. But some books have a much more complex history. A writer may borrow material from other sources. A writer may give his or her manuscript to someone to edit, or there may be several editors. Someone may find a person's written but unfinished notes and publish them after some editing. There are books which are the published notes that someone took at public lectures. Sometimes people write books not under their own name, but under a pseudonym. Or a book may pass through several editions; we speak of a new and revised edition. The original writer may be responsible for additions to his or her book; yet, after the author's death, someone else may make further additions to the work. At times, therefore, it becomes difficult to know who wrote what. If we have access to several editions of the same book, we can compare them and so discover what is the original text and what are the additions.

All this also applies to the biblical books, which generally have a complex history. It is particularly evident in the paradise story, a text taken from the book called Genesis. Any intelligent reader will soon discover the complexity of that book, which starts with a story of how God created the universe in six days, then rested on the seventh day (1:1–2:4a). The text then goes on: "At the time when Yahweh God made earth and heaven there was as yet no wild bush on the earth… nor was there any man to till the soil" (2:4b-5). This is rather difficult to understand since the reader has just heard about the creation of the plants (1:11-13) and of man (1:26-27).

By looking more carefully, one notices many differences at the level of the vocabulary. The first account speaks about "God," and about "heaven and earth" (1:1; 2:1, 4a), the second about "Yahweh God," and about "earth and heaven" (2:4b). The style is also different. The first story is highly structured, repeating the same formulas, while the second appears to be more a nice story that people liked to tell. Finally, the theology of the two accounts is very different. The first story stresses the transcendence of God, who does not seem to do anything other than give orders from heaven: "Let there be…," while the second story stresses the immanence of God, who is down on earth, who works with his hands to fashion man from the dust, and who speaks to people. One must conclude that we are in the presence of two texts of different origin.

The paradise story itself presents difficulties for the critical reader. Normally the texts in Genesis speak of

"God" or of "Yahweh," this text uses the double name "Yahweh God." The story apparently contains some repetitions. "Yahweh God planted a garden... and there he put the man he had fashioned" (2:8) and a bit later, the man who was already in the garden is put there a second time, "Yahweh God took the man and settled him in the garden of Eden" (2:15). The text says that the tree of life is in the middle of the garden (2:9), but later it appears that the tree of the knowledge of good and evil is in the middle (3:3). The man and the woman "sewed fig-leaves together to make themselves loin-cloths" (3:7), thus they are clothed. When God appears, they hide and the man replies to God who is searching for them, "I was afraid because I was naked, so I hid" (3:10). So God gives them other clothes, "Yahweh God made clothes out of skins for the man and his wife, and they put them on" (3:21), over their fig-leaves perhaps.

There are also other irregularities in the story. The text says that if they eat of the forbidden tree they will die, "for on the day you eat of it, you shall most surely die" (2:17). But after they have eaten of the tree, they do not die that day (3:7). It appears that the author of the story has used other material, other sources that he has put together to form the present story. Among the many proposed solutions, many scholars now accept the following one.[1] At times in the story everything seems to

---

[1] C. Westermann, *Genesis* (*Biblischer Kommentar Altes Testament,* 1) (Neukirchen-Vluyn: Neukirchener Verlag, 1974), pp. 255-67, translation: J. J. Scullion, *Genesis 1-11: A Commentary* (Minneapolis: Augsburg Publishing House, 1984).

be in abundance in the garden (2:9), but at times the human person has to work to feed himself (2:15). In several verses, referring to the creation of the man and the woman, God is the sole acting person and speaks only to himself (2:18); the human person is passive. In other verses, speaking of a garden, the human person is the acting person and God enters into dialogue with the human person. All this points to the existence of two independent stories: one is a creation story (2:4b-6, 7-8, 15, 18-24), the other is a paradise story (2:9, 16-17, 25; 3:1-24). Since both stories speak of a garden, the author has combined them into one story.

II. Author-centred Interpretations of Genesis 2–3

The preceding illustrates that in order to discover the meaning intended by the author a great deal of research has to be done about the world behind the text. The important question has not yet been asked: Who is the author of the paradise story? If we want to find his or her intention, we should know who the author is.

1. Moses Is the Author

For a long time the answer to the question of the author's identity was very simple. People believed that Moses was the author of the Torah, or the Pentateuch, and thus of the book Genesis and consequently of the paradise story. The text raised no problems because it was read as *history*. Moses wrote about a unique event in the life of two historical individuals, the first man and the first woman of the human race. Because of their rather childish sin of eating an apple (even if the text never speaks of an apple), all humans now are born with original sin. This raised all kinds of theological discussions, such as what would happen to children who died without baptism and thus with original sin; theologians created limbo for them. This type of historical reading led to a *moralizing* reading of the text, in which people were warned not to follow the example of the first couple. People were strongly advised to avoid satan, to beware of pride, of disobedience and, above all, to avoid sexual misbehaviour and to be careful of the danger of woman. The lack of feeling of shame in society especially in the sexual domain was severely criticized.

2. Not Moses, but the Yahwist Is the Author

The literary genre of the paradise story, as we have seen, is not history at all, but myth. This myth consequently does not speak about the first man and woman and their behaviour, but about the universal human condition. The story presents how people were, are and will be. It speaks about your behaviour and mine. But, as we have seen, even if an author speaks about universal truths, the contexts in which that writer lives will influence what he or she says. And thus the question remains: Who wrote the story?

We noticed that the creation story (1:1–2:4a) is very different from the paradise story (2:4b–3:24). Each one has its own literary and theological characteristics. But these same characteristics reappear in other texts in the Pentateuch and this has led scholars to conclude that there are four different layers, or traditions, in the Pentateuch. One of them is called the *Yahwist* because that tradition uses the divine name 'Yahweh' right from the beginning of Genesis, even though in fact that name was revealed to Moses only at the time of the Exodus (Ex 3:13-15). The paradise story is thus believed to have been written by the Yahwist. It is an artificial name to refer to an author whose real name is unknown.

Details in a text often reveal where the text comes from and when it was written. For example, if one reads a book on the history of Canada, it will be rather easy to discover if the author is of Native or of European descent, and if he or she is a French-Canadian or an English-Canadian. If, in a text, the city referred to is always Toronto, there is a good chance that this text comes from the Toronto region and not from Brussels. If a text speaks of jet fighters, I know that it was not written in the Middle Ages.

By reading all the texts of the Pentateuch belonging to the yahwistic tradition, scholars have tried to determine where the Yahwist was living and when. Based on clues from the text, they suggest that he lived in Judah, in the south, and that he must have written during the time of King David, or more probably during the time of Solomon, in the second part of the tenth century before Christ. We have a great deal of information about that historical period, thanks to the historical books of the Bible and to extra-biblical data, which makes it possible to reconstruct the geographical, historical, cultural, social and political contexts which must have had their impact on the Yahwist when he wrote the paradise story or when he reworked some of the sources he may have used.

The figure of David and his life were still very fresh in the memory of the people. David even became the ideal king with whom other kings later would be compared and measured. Another literary work from that same period is the story of David's family, the so-called succession story (2 Sam 9-20; 1 Kings 1-2). A comparison between some texts related to David and the paradise story reveals remarkable similarities. One gets the impression that the Yahwist wrote a real prophecy of the past, that he projected the experience of David into what happened in the beginning. W. Brueggemann suggests that David's experience becomes the model to describe the experience of all humans or of universal human nature.[2] The parallels between David and Adam are striking (we use the name Adam to simplify the comparison, even if the word *adam* in the paradise story means humanity or man and is not yet a proper name).

The first set of parallels is between the oracle of Nathan addressed to David, called the davidic covenant (2 Sam 7), which describes God's gifts to David and the first part of the paradise story (Gen 2), which describes God's gifts to Adam.

---

[2] W. Brueggemann, "David and His Theologian," in *Catholic Biblical Quarterly*, 30 (1968), pp. 156-81.

Both David and Adam are raised from nothing to something. David was of simple origin, a shepherd, before becoming king. Yahweh, through the prophet Nathan, says to David, "I took you from the pasture, from following the sheep, to be leader of my people Israel" (2 Sam 7:8). The paradise story stresses in a similar way the humble origin of Adam, "Yahweh God fashioned man of dust from the soil. Then he breathed into his nostrils a breath of life, and thus man became a living being" (Gen 2:7). It is interesting to note that this same expression is used later in the context of the enthronement of King Baasha of Israel, "I raised you from the dust and made you leader of my people Israel" (1 Kings 16:2).

Both David and Adam live in a special place. In the same oracle of Nathan, the prophet goes on to remind David how Yahweh, after raising him to be king, has been with him in his expeditions, has defeated all his enemies and thus, "I will provide a place for my people Israel; I will plant them there and they shall dwell in that place..." (2 Sam 7:10). After creating Adam, "Yahweh God planted a garden in Eden which is in the east, and there he put the man he had fashioned" (Gen 2:8) and a little further, "Yahweh God took the man and settled him in the garden of Eden..." (2:15).

Both David and Adam have responsibility for that place. David, as king, is called to care for the people of Yahweh, "I took you... to be leader of my people Israel" (2 Sam 7:8). Adam is called to care for the garden, "Yahweh God took the man and settled him in the garden of Eden to cultivate and take care of it" (Gen 2:15).

Both David and Adam enjoy great freedom, but at the same time a limit is set. Yahweh promises David that he will always be with him and his dynasty, "I will be a father to him and he a son to me; if he does evil, I will punish him with the rod such as humans use, with strokes such as humankind gives" (2 Sam 7:14). Adam's freedom also knows a limitation, "You may eat indeed of all the trees in the garden. Nevertheless of the tree of the knowledge of good and evil you are not to eat, for on the day you eat of it you shall most surely die" (Gen 2:16-17).

Both David and Adam receive sovereignty over other creatures. King David receives power over his enemies, "I have been with you on all your expeditions; I have cut off all your enemies before you" (2 Sam 7:9). Adam receives power over the animals, "So from the soil Yahweh God fashioned all the wild beasts and all the birds of heaven. These he brought to the man to see what he would call them; each one was to bear the name the man would give it. The man gave names to all the cattle, all the birds of heaven and all the wild beasts" (Gen 2:19-20).

A second set of parallels occurs between the story of David's sin with Bathsheba, describing his response to God's favours (2 Sam 11-12), and the second part of the paradise story (Gen 3), Adam and Eve's sin, describing their response to God's favours.

Both David and Adam are attracted to the one person or object which is forbidden. David is attracted to the beautiful woman, he desires her, takes her and sleeps with her, "(David) saw... a woman bathing; the woman was very beautiful. David made inquiries... David sent messengers and had her brought... and he slept with her" (2 Sam 11:2-4). The action of Adam and Eve follows the same structure: first the recognition of beauty, then the desire, then the taking and finally the eating, "The woman saw that the tree was good to eat and pleasing to the eye, and that it was desirable for the knowledge that it could give. So she took some of its fruit and ate it. She gave some also to her husband who was with her, and he ate" (Gen 3:6).

Both David and Adam are conscious of having done something wrong. After Nathan's intervention, David confesses his sin, "I have sinned against Yahweh" (2 Sam 12:13). The eyes of Adam and Eve open after their sin (Gen 3:7) and when Yahweh appears, they hide, and Adam replies to Yahweh, "I heard the sound of you in the garden; I was afraid because I was naked, so I hid" (3:10).

God judges both David and Adam. David, who did not understand that Nathan was telling him a parable, pronounces his own death penalty, "the man who did this deserves to die" (2 Sam 12:5). The death penalty, however, is not executed, "Yahweh, for his part, forgives your sin; you are not to die" (12:13; the child to be born will die, 12:14), but there will be a punishment, "So now the sword will never be far from your House" (12:10). In Adam and Eve's case, something similar happens. The penalty for eating of the tree was clearly death, "for on the day you eat of it you shall most surely die" (Gen 2:17). This time also the death penalty is not executed after the transgression, but Eve and Adam receive their punishment (3:16, 17-19); the story even speaks of a "sword" (3:24).

For both David and Adam hope is revived with the birth of a child. After the child of David and Bathsheba died, "David consoled his wife Bathsheba. He went to her and slept with her. She conceived and gave birth to a son whom she named Solomon. Yahweh loved him" (2 Sam 12:24). Once more we notice the strong similarity with Adam and Eve after the death of their child Abel, "Adam had intercourse with his wife, and she gave birth to a son whom she named Seth, 'because God has granted me other offspring' she said 'in place of Abel, since Cain has killed him'" (Gen 4:25).

The Yahwist has seen how God blessed David in the most exceptional ways. How this king, who, humanly speaking, had everything he could wish for, still wanted what he could not have, and so sinned, bringing terrible disaster upon himself through God's judgment. God's grace, however, transcended his judgment and God showed his graciousness through a new son. What the Yahwist had noticed in the life of the king becomes for him the model of how God treats Adam and Eve, in other words how God acts with everybody. Every human person is a king.

3. Not Only the Yahwist, but Several Authors

Scholars used to explain the repetitions in the paradise story by pointing to the sources which the Yahwist would have used when he compiled his story. But J. Vermeylen now suggests that some of these repetitions cannot be explained by sources used by the Yahwist, but are explained rather by subsequent redactions of the text, later than the Yahwist.[3]

Vermeylen suggests that the section Genesis 3:14-21 repeats three things which are mentioned elsewhere in the story: a) the individual punishments of each actor of the story (3:14-19) duplicate the punishment of their expulsion from the garden (3:22-24); b) the giving of the name "Eve" (3:20) duplicates the first name-giving as "woman" (2:23); c) the clothing with skins (3:21) duplicates the clothing with leaves (3:7).

After a careful study of the vocabulary and of the theology contained in this section, Vermeylen concludes that these verses have nothing in common with other texts belonging to the Yahwist, but are of a later date, and are thus redactional. The story of paradise is not written simply by one author, the Yahwist, but is the result of a long process in which Vermeylen distinguishes four stages: the archaic story, the yahwistic story, the deuteronomistic story, and the priestly (?) additions.

The archaic story: In the earliest phase, a myth spoke only about God and man, and did not mention a serpent or a woman. The man is expelled from paradise, which is God's domain, and thus also from the tree of life growing in the middle of the garden. It illustrates man's inferior mortal condition. This story, which probably existed in oral form only, cannot be reconstructed with precision.

---

[3] J. Vermeylen, "Le récit du paradis et la question des origines du Pentateuque," in *Bijdragen*, 41 (1980), pp. 230-50.

The yahwistic story: The Yahwist at the time of Solomon put this myth into writing and enriched it with the motifs of the tree of the knowledge of good and evil, of the woman and of the serpent. Basically, he gave the story its present form, which speaks about the universal human condition. Humanity in its desire to become like God is expelled from the garden.

The deuteronomistic story: A deuteronomistic redactor reworked the yahwistic story during the exile and introduced — through the individual punishments of each actor, the serpent (3:14), the woman (3:16), the man (3:17-18a, 19) — the interrelated concepts of individual human responsibility and divine justice. The deuteronomistic redactor wanted to correct the global expulsion from the garden, so each is punished according to his or her deeds.

The universal myth has been replaced by history. The story no longer speaks of the universal but of the contingent, the example of the two first human beings, Adam and Eve (3:20). This history is supposed to contribute to confidence in a God who is accused of having arbitrarily rejected his people in exile. But God shows his graciousness to Adam and Eve (3:21). The deuteronomistic writer thus introduces the concepts of human culpability, just divine punishment and grace.

The last (priestly?) additions: Two elements are later than the deuteronomistic edition, 3:15 and 3:18b. They seem to interpret the story in relation to the situation of the pious community of the second temple, confronted with the hostility of the "impious" (3:15). These are probably from the final redactor of the Pentateuch.

This reconstruction of the development of the account conflicts with Brueggemann's proposition that the Yahwist wrote the paradise story with the story of David in mind. Brueggemann suggests, for instance, that the Yahwist used the punishment of David (2 Sam 12:10) to speak of the punishment of Eve and Adam (Gen 3:16, 17-19). However, according to Vermeylen, these verses are not from the Yahwist but from the deuteronomistic writer, who wrote much later at the time of the exile.

Vermeylen's complex reconstruction, as anyone can see, remains pure hypothesis and will never receive unanimous acceptance by scholars. Can we ever be certain that half a verse (3:18b) belongs to a totally different period or comes from a totally different writer?

4. Was There Ever a Yahwist?

Critical studies have shown that Moses could not be the author of the paradise story and have suggested that the Yahwist was the author of the whole paradise story (Westermann, Brueggemann), or at least of one stage of its composition (Vermeylen). But what do we really know about the Yahwist? His proper name is unknown, and we have to guess about who he was and what he did in life. Was he a royal scribe, a priest, a farmer, a man or a woman, young or old, rich or poor? All these details could make a significant difference for the understanding of the paradise story.

And the critical studies go on and on. R. Rendtorff[4] wonders about the existence of what has been called the yahwistic tradition. Other scholars, for instance J. Van Seters,[5] while still accepting the yahwistic tradition, do not date it from the time of Solomon, but from the time of the exile, which totally invalidates Brueggemann's beautiful exegesis and also Vermeylen's.

III. Advantages and Limitations of an Author-centred Interpretation

What we have described is the approach taken by the *historical-critical method.* This method, or methods, tries to uncover the world behind the text. *Form criticism* tries to determine the literary genre of the text and its *Sitz im Leben*, the life situation in which the text originates. *Source criticism* attempts to discover the sources that the writer may have used. *Redaction criticism,* such as practised by Vermeylen, wants to discover the different redactions of a text which have tried to adapt the text to the ever-changing circumstances of life. Despite all the effort and all the research, we are still trying to identify the writer. And until we know the writer, how are we ever going to find the so-called intention of the writer?

We want to know what the writer had in mind when he or she wrote; in other words we are looking for the

---

[4] R. Rendtorff, "The 'Yahwist' as Theologian? The Dilemma of Pentateuchal Criticism," in *Journal for the Study of the Old Testament,* 3 (1977), pp. 2-10.

[5] J. Van Seters, *Abraham in History and Tradition* (New Haven/ London: Yale University Press, 1975).

conscious intention of the writer. But as we all know, our unconscious has an impact on all we do. Freud has certainly made us aware of this. When an author writes, the unconscious is working too and influences the text. The reader will thus have to read between the lines for the feelings, the dispositions, the reasons, the motifs, the effects and the consequences of what has been written. Studies using psychological or psychoanalytical methods try to uncover all of that, and they can be applied to the paradise story.[6] But how can we ever reach this stage if we do not know the writer?

Even if one day we were able to determine with precision who the writers of all the biblical texts were, even then a basic question would remain. Who could even dream of discovering what a writer really had in mind, unless we could ask the person? And of course, all the biblical authors are long since dead. We have difficulty enough understanding ourselves, how then could we ever understand another person totally! It is, therefore, not surprising that in biblical studies, since most of the writers are unknown, people start to wonder if the methods used until now are really effective. Instead of continuing to favour the author, shouldn't we rather be looking at the two other actors in the reading process: the reader and the text?

---

[6] M. Balmary, *Le sacrifice interdit: Freud et la Bible* (Paris: B.Grasset, 1986), chap. X: "En Eden," pp. 235-71; E. Drewermann, "Angoisse et faute dans le récit yahviste de la chute (Gen 3,15)," in *Concilium*, 113 (1976), pp. 71-82; X. Thévenot, "Emmaüs, une nouvelle Genèse? Une lecture psychanalytique de Genèse 2-3 et Luc 24,13-25," in *Mélanges de science religieuse*, 37 (1980), pp. 3-18.

It would, however, be disastrous to abandon our search for the world behind the text because of the impossibility of uncovering the precise author and his or her intention. A text is the product of a writer, and the writer is a product of his or her world. Even if we cannot identify the author, we know that he or she lived in another world, and even if we do not know the precise circumstances of his or her life, there are certain aspects of this historical research which remain valid.

The world of the Bible is different from our world. For instance, the word 'brother' has a broader meaning in the Bible than it has for Canadians today. To avoid misunderstandings, we must be aware of the distance between our world and the world behind the text. Much of this work is done for the ordinary Bible reader by the translators. A good translation transfers one culture into another culture, a difficult and delicate but indispensable task. Furthermore, we must be aware that any translation is an interpretation, and when we make an interpretation of a translation, we have added another level of interpretation. A good Bible includes footnotes, chronological tables and maps to help the reader understand the geographical, historical, political, social and linguistic contexts of the biblical texts. But even with all the richness provided by a good translation, the reader must realize that the question, *What did the writer — consciously or unconsciously — have in mind?* will never be settled. All possible answers will always remain tentative and incomplete.[7]

---

[7] W. Vogels, "Les limites de la méthode historico-critique," in *Laval théologique et philosophique*, 36 (1980), pp. 173-94.

II

The Reader Gives Meaning

I. Presuppositions and Theory of a Reader-centred Interpretation

There is no doubt that without a writer there would be no book, but that person wrote so that others might read. Without a reader, there is no communication and a book is useless: it is just a certain number of pages of paper. A book that is not read is stacked on a library shelf or stored in a museum. The book is dead, or rather, the book is in 'hibernation,' waiting to receive life from a reader. The reader will interpret that book, revive it, resurrect it, give it meaning. It has been said that each reader rewrites the book.

We have been inclined to stress the importance of the author, after all his or her name appears on the cover, but the reader is equally important. Even to the point that writers have to take very seriously into account the readers for whom they are writing. Writers often identify the audience they want to address and adjust to that audience. Writers may address their peers, scholars, or the larger public. Publishers ask writers who the intended audience is as this affects the publicity. Without the author there is no book, but without the reader there is no living book.

In an author-centred interpretation of the text, the degree of difficulty involved in the interpretation depends, as we have seen, on two basic variables: one related to the identity of the author and the other to what and how that person wrote. A reader-centred interpretation too is determined by two variables: one related to the clarity of the text, the other to the identity of the reader.

1. The Clarity of the Text

Any person who has written a text knows how difficult it is to be clear. We realize this even more if we have to write something very important. So we are inclined, after we have written the text, to reread it and to correct it, because we are not satisfied with a particular word or with the structure of a sentence. After we have corrected our first draft, we may reread it again and make further changes. And we could go on like this for a very long time, especially now, since with word processors it has become so easy to correct and change our texts. And still, we cannot go on correcting and changing that text for the rest of our lives. At a certain moment the writer must decide that this is the final text. In a sense, as writers we have to accept that what we write can never totally and perfectly express what we want to say. We try. The writer then gives the text to the printer and now it has become too late to change anything.

If the writer is lucky, the book will come into the hands of a reader who will start interpreting. We all have had the experience of receiving a letter from a good friend and, while reading it, thinking, "I am sure that this is not what my friend wanted to say." We know the friend so well that we realize that he or she has forgotten a comma, a word or whatever. There is what we call a 'gap' in the text. The example of a letter from a friend represents the most optimal conditions of communication.

However, these difficulties become more serious when writer and reader are strangers to each other. We may have written a letter to someone we do not know personally and when we receive the answer, realize that the person did not understand at all what we had in mind. We may be upset, but by rereading a copy of our original letter, we sometimes have to admit that, indeed, we were not clear enough or that the letter could be understood in a different way from what we had intended. These examples, based upon our common human experience, illustrate that there may be a difference between what the writer intended and what the text says. If the writer is still alive, he or she may protest, but if the writer is dead, like of course all biblical writers are, there will be no protest. How could I ever know if 'Matthew' forgot a comma?

Besides the difficulty of writing clearly, a good author must — and wants to — give the reader some freedom. First of all, it would be impossible for a writer to say everything; secondly, it would become extremely boring to read everything neatly spelled out. A good writer leaves some work to the reader's creativity.

The lack of clarity in a text is caused in part by the gaps in the text, which the reader has to fill in. We do not speak here of some special difficulties of biblical texts which are due to the long transmission of these texts. Before printing existed, people were obliged to copy the texts by hand, which of course explains why numerous errors, conscious or unconscious, were introduced into the text. A special science or art, called *textual criticism,* concentrates on the restoration of the original text. The gaps we are speaking of here are those which are simply part of writing.[1]

a. Grammatical and Syntactical Gaps

Some gaps are due to the inherent ambiguity of language. The often quoted example is: "John makes love with his wife twice a week. So does Charles." This sentence is indeed open to two very different interpretations. Does Charles make love with his wife twice a week as John does with his wife? Or does Charles make love twice a week with John's wife? The two interpretations are possible and one notices the very different implica-

[1] Inspired by W. R. Tate, *Biblical Interpretation: An Integrated Approach* (Peabody, Massachusetts: Hendrickson Publishers, 1991), pp. 151-59.

tions. Similarly, does 'the love of God' mean the love that God has for us or is it the love we give God? The context may provide the answer; it may not. The reader has to fill in such gaps.

A frequent syntactical gap arises from the confusion about a pronoun's antecedent. A good example of this can be found in the paradise story in a highly disputed verse, sometimes called the proto-evangelium or the first proclamation of the good news (Gen 3:15).[2] At the end of the verse, the text uses the pronoun *hu*, which may mean the masculine 'he,' or the neutral 'it.'[3] To whom or to what does this refer? The text speaks of the battle which starts in paradise between the serpent and the woman (v. 15a), continues between the offspring of the serpent and the offspring of the woman (v. 15b) and ends with "*hu* [he or it] will *shuph* your head and you will *shuph* [his or its] heel" (v. 15c). If one translates using the neutral, "It will crush your head and you will strike its heel" *(Jerusalem Bible),* then the final stage of the battle is between the offspring of the woman and the serpent. But if one translates using the masculine, "He will strike at your head, while you strike at his heel" *(New American Bible,* similar *Revised Standard Version),* then, at the final stage of the battle with the serpent, an individual male actor appears, who then is called the messiah.

---

[2] W. Vogels, "Lezingen van het zogenoemde 'Proto-evangelie' (Gen 3,15)," in *Sacerdos*, 53 (1986), pp. 351-66, translation: W. Vogels, "Das sog. 'Proto-Evangelium' (Gen 3,15): Verschiedene Arten, den Text zu lesen," in *Theologie der Gegenwart*, 29 (1986), pp. 195-203.

[3] See above, pp. 20-21.

Another kind of gap occurs when a text uses a word which has two meanings. The beginning of the paradise story speaks of the creation of *ha-adam* (2:7). The word *adam*, which means humanity, human person or man (male), appears here with the article *ha*. Does this verse therefore describe the creation of humanity or of a human person, or the creation of the man (male) since the woman is created later (2:21)? After God decides that it is not good for this *ha-adam* to be alone and creating the animals, the text concludes, "But no helpmate suitable for *adam* was found for him" (2:20).[4] The word *adam* appears now without the article. Does the text now mean that there is no suitable helpmate found 'for *a* human person,' 'for *a* man,' or 'for *the* human person,' 'for *the* man,' or even 'for Adam,' since *adam* without the article becomes later the proper name of the first man whose wife is Eve (see Gen 4:25)? The choices made at this stage clearly affect the meaning of the text. We will return to this discussion later.

The so-called proto-evangelium (3:15) provides another example in the paradise story of a gap caused by the double meaning of a word. The difficulty is once more in the last part of the verse, "[he or it] will *shuph* your head, and you shall *shuph* [his or its] heel" (v. 15c). This verb *shuph,* used twice in this verse, is very rare in the Hebrew Bible; it is found in only two other texts,

---

[4] D. Barthélemy, " 'Pour un homme', 'Pour l'homme' ou 'Pour Adam'? (Gen 2,20)," in M. Carrez, J. Doré, and P. Grelot (ed.), *De la Tôrah au Messie: Etudes d'exégèse et d'herméneutique bibliques offertes à Henri Cazelles* (Paris: Desclée, 1981), pp. 47-53.

Psalm 139:11 (but the text is corrupt) and Job 9:17. Its meaning, therefore, is not easy to determine.

Experts have compared this verb with an Akkadian verb, *shapu,* which means 'to trample or to crush under the foot.' This would fit the first part of the verse, to crush the head, but is rather difficult to reconcile with the heel in the second part. Scholars also suggest the similarity with another Hebrew verb, *sha'aph*, which has a double meaning, 'crush' and 'watch.'

Some translators decide that the verb must have the same meaning in both parts of the verse, "He shall *bruise* your head, and you shall *bruise* his heel" *(Revised Standard Version).* In such a translation the battle may seem hopeless since, while the offspring of the woman or the male actor crushes the head of the serpent, the serpent strikes the heel of its adversary, and we all know that a serpent bite is enough to kill. The fight ends without victor since both die in their struggle. Some maintain that there is hope, since to crush the head of someone is really the end of that person.

Other translators wonder if the text is not playing on the double meaning of the verb, since in this same story there are other word plays. They suggest that the verse should be translated: "[It or he] shall crush your head, and you shall watch [its or his] heel." The offspring of the woman or the male actor crushes the head of the serpent which is watching its adversary and is ready to attack, but is too late. In this case, the text certainly speaks of hope. It would then indeed be the proclamation of good news for humanity. If one opts simultaneously for the masculine translation of *hu* by 'he,' the text then says that this victory over evil will be brought about by the messiah. The text can then be understood as a messianic text.

b. Poetic and Literary Gaps

Between the sentences of a text there are all kinds of connections. Some of these are not necessarily stated explicitly; they are there implicitly. The writer may make huge leaps and leave the task of making the connections, of filling in the gaps, to the creativity and imagination of the reader.

U. Eco gives an excellent example of this.[5] Person A says: "I am out of petrol" (North Americans would say gas). B answers: "There is a garage round the corner." These two very short sentences in fact hide a whole story. "A needs petrol and B wants to help him. B knows that A knows that usually garages sell petrol, knows that there is a garage round the corner, and knows (or hopes) that this garage is open and has petrol to sell. So he informs A about the location of the garage. Will or will not A follow successfully the suggestion of B?" Thus the story has many implicit connections, but has also some suspense.

The reader, having read the beginning of a story, may wonder about the next step of the story. He or she may question what will happen next and may foresee different possibilities. The reading of that next step of the story reveals which possibility the writer has chosen. Some-

---

5 U. Eco, *The Role of the Reader: Explorations in the Semiotics of Texts* (Bloomington: Indiana University Press, 1979), p. 29.

thing at a certain point in the story may force the reader to correct his or her first interpretation. The end of the story confirms or contradicts the solutions adopted by the reader all along the way. It is, therefore, not surprising that some people first read the end of a book. Difficult texts sometimes need to be read twice or even more often and, at times, backwards.

But all this effort on the part of the reader does not necessarily exclude the ambiguity of the text. Some texts are and remain mysterious; some writers are deliberately ambiguous. Brueggemann suggests, as we have seen, that the Yahwist in his paradise story was inspired by what happened in the life of David, as told in the succession narrative.[6] There is a lot of ambiguity in the story of David's sin with Bathsheba (2 Sam 11). The text says, "It happened towards evening when David had risen from his couch and was strolling on the palace roof, that he saw from the roof a woman bathing; the woman was very beautiful" (v. 2). Is David the bad guy, is he a perverse voyeur? Or is Bathsheba the bad girl? She must have known that people could see her. Is she the type of woman who likes to provoke men? The text leaves the reader with the question and moves on, "Then David sent messengers and had her brought. She came to him, and he slept with her..." (v. 4). This verse makes the story even more mysterious. When the text says that the king "had her brought," it appears that the woman is the victim, exploited by a man abusing his position of power. But the

---

6 W. Brueggemann, "David and His Theologian," in *Catholic Biblical Quarterly*, 30 (1968), pp. 156-81; see above, pp. 32-36.

text says at the same time "she came to him." The verb is definitely active. Nothing in the text says that she objected; on the contrary "she came." She may have enjoyed having this affair with the king.

We encounter the same type of ambiguity in the paradise story in the text of the sin of Adam and Eve, which according to Brueggemann is inspired by the David text. "The woman saw that the tree was good to eat and pleasing to the eye, and that it was desirable for the knowledge that it could give. So she took some of its fruit and ate it" (Gen 3:6), but that same verse goes on, "She gave some also to her husband who was with her, and he ate it." Is Eve the evil woman who has tempted her husband? On the other hand, she does not say one single word and the text states explicitly that he "was with her." Does it not appear rather to be a common decision, a common sin? These two examples of David–Bathsheba and Adam–Eve show that readers will probably make decisions according to factors outside the text. A male or female chauvinist, for instance, will certainly read these two texts very differently and come up with different answers to the questions raised. And this leads us to the second variable in a reader-centred interpretation.

2. The World of the Reader

The author of a book, as we have seen, is a human person living in a particular time, at a particular place, in particular cultural, ideological, historical, linguistic, social and political conditions. We spoke of a whole world *behind the text.* This applies equally to the reader.

The reader is not an innocent bystander, because the person who reads or rewrites the text is also conditioned by similar factors. We can now speak of the world of the reader, the world *in front of the text.* Readers bring their own world to the text, their various life experiences, their presuppositions, their ideologies, their interests, their competencies and the methods they use. The questions readers ask of the text come from their own interests.

Let us take once more the example of the letter from a good friend. When I read that letter quickly when I arrive home after work, I certainly get something out of it. If I reread this letter later in the evening when I have more time, I may find new things. If I reread the letter a few weeks later as I prepare to answer my friend, it may happen that I suddenly discover something I had not noticed before. And if my friend dies, that letter over the years may again speak to me in various new ways.

Many factors in the reader affect his or her understanding of the text. Even after reading a text dozens of times or for many years, there are always aspects of the text which were not noticed before or speak now in a different way. Reading is dynamic, open-ended, always open to change, correction, or enrichment, because the reader changes. People often say that they search for the objective meaning of a text, but reading is always subjective. We all read through our own glasses, nobody can avoid this. This explains why the understanding of the same text changes for us over the years, and also why the same text, read by different people, can mean so many different things to them.

The reading of the Bible does not escape this principle. A person in the midst of personal suffering will read the Book of Job very differently from when he or she was studying it at university. The differences in the synoptic gospels illustrate that this principle was already at work when people were listening to Jesus' preaching. In the gospel of Matthew we read as first beatitude, "How happy are the poor in spirit" (Matthew 5:3), while in Luke this is formulated differently, "How happy are you who are poor" (Luke 6:20). This might correspond to how people in North America and people in South America would have understood Jesus' preaching. It is, therefore, impossible to give 'the' meaning of the Bible or of a biblical text. It has different meanings to different people in different places at different times.

New scientific discoveries often force readers of the Bible to question some of their most accepted earlier interpretations. New sensitivities in society, for instance, on the relationship between men and women, on social justice, or on ecology, affect the present reader, who may thus discover aspects of biblical texts which were hidden until now. Since society changes, the individuals in that society change and thus their understanding of that same old book changes. Four examples illustrate how this affects the reading of the paradise story.

II. Reader-centred Interpretations of Genesis 2–3

1. Pre-scientific or Scientific Informed Reading

In the past, and still today, many readers have never questioned what the paradise story says about the creation of man and woman. The text is very simple, "God fashioned man of the dust from the soil. Then he breathed into his nostrils a breath of life" (Gen 2:7), and a bit later, "Yahweh God made the man fall into a deep sleep. And while he slept, he took one of his ribs and enclosed it in flesh" (2:21). This last verse became important in the mid-1800s in the discussion concerning the morality of anaesthetics. James Young Simpson, a Scottish physician, believed that the best proof of the morality of using anaesthetics was in the Bible. Since God had already practised anaesthesia on Adam — so that he could take the rib to make the woman, "Yahweh God made the man fall into a deep sleep. And while he slept…" — the use of anaesthetics could not possibly be immoral.

When science started to suggest theories about the origin of the world and of humanity, a scientific informed reader was forced to return to the Bible and to examine his or her interpretation. The biblical explanation presented in the paradise story that humanity was fashioned of dust from the soil is very different from the scientific explanation of the origin of humanity through evolution. Our great-great-grandparents may have been monkeys! Or perhaps humans and monkeys are 'cousins' descended from a common ancestor who no longer walked on four legs.

Such theories made us aware that the biblical text is obviously not a scientific text in the modern sense of the word. It is not trying to explain scientifically how we were created, but speaks rather in a symbolic way. When we die, we stop breathing; we speak of the 'last breath.' And what is left turns to dust. This explains why the biblical author used this image: it illustrates clearly that there is something in us which makes us belong to the earth, "of dust from the soil," but that there is also something in us which makes us live. We participate in that life that only God has in fullness. The image of the rib expresses that man and woman share in the same nature. Scholars have suggested that the writer chose the rib because, in Sumerian, the word 'ti' means 'rib' *and* 'life.' In French, one could play on the words 'côte' (rib) and 'côté' (side).

Scientific discoveries have forced the reader to reconsider his or her previous simplistic interpretation of the paradise story and, far from destroying the richness of the Bible, have led to a better and deeper understanding.

2. Jewish or Christian Reading

There is no such thing as a Jewish, as opposed to a Christian, reading of the Bible. Jews and Christians do not necessarily use different methods or approaches. Many Jewish scholars interpret the Bible the way Christian scholars do, and vice-versa. Still, on some points, the religious affiliation of the scholar influences interpretation. The most obvious difference is that the Jewish believer does not include what Christians call the New Testament in his or her Bible. The corpus of books for the Jewish believer is different from the corpus accepted by the Christian believer and this certainly affects the interpretation of some texts. This can be illustrated by an example from the paradise story.

We have referred to the Genesis verse about the second part of the serpent's punishment and to the discussion on the translation of *hu* by the masculine 'he' or the neutral 'it' (3:15).[7] A purely literary critic with no religious affiliation, who studies this text simply as an ancient text, will most probably conclude that this *hu* refers to what immediately precedes, the offspring of the woman, and thus translate by 'it.' This seems the most obvious meaning. A believer may opt for the same interpretation. But some, as we have seen, informed by other biblical texts, are aware of Israel's belief in the coming of the messiah and may opt for the masculine translation 'he.' They may even point to the fact that the Septuagint, the Greek translation of the Bible made by Jews in the third or second century before Christ, opted for this masculine meaning. Some Jewish and Christian interpreters may thus consider this text a messianic text.

This is where interpretations diverge. For the Jewish believer, that messiah is still to come, still awaited. For the Christian believer, that messiah has come in the person of Jesus; thus he or she may even give a christo-

[7] See above, p. 47.

logical meaning to this verse. The Christian tradition has sometimes given a mariological meaning to this verse — think of the statues where Mary crushes the head of the serpent — which of course is found more frequently in Catholic than in Protestant milieus.

3. Male or Female Reading

One recent change in Western society is our greater awareness of the numerous injustices done to women. We have become more aware of the fact that we have looked at the world mostly from the male perspective and neglected the female perspective. This new sensitivity affects our understanding of texts in general, and of biblical texts in particular. The paradise story provides an excellent case study of how this sensitivity affects, corrects and enriches the interpretation of this story.

It is a most exciting experience to go through the history of the exegesis of the section in the paradise story which speaks of the creation of the woman and of the relationship between man and woman (2:18-20).[8] From among the numerous studies, let us begin with one which summarizes rather well the position of most exegetes of the 1960s.

J. De Fraine gives the following commentary on Genesis 2:18-24:

---

[8] W. Vogels, " 'It Is not Good that the 'Mensch' Should Be Alone; I Will Make Him/Her a Helper Fit for Him/Her' (Gen 2:18)," in *Eglise et théologie*, 9 (1978), pp. 9-35.

> Whatever may have been the nature of that part of Adam's body which was taken from him, the meaning of the narrative is clear enough: man and woman constitute an indissoluble unity. The woman can be thought of only as a part of the man. By means of this image, three ideas are expressed:
>
> 1) The solid bond between husband and wife... (Eph 5:28-29).
>
> 2) The special dignity of the man: "because a husband is head of the wife" (Eph 5:23). For this reason: "woman is the glory of man" (1 Cor 11:7). On the other hand she must be subject to him... (1 Tm 2:12-13).
>
> 3) The natural equality between man and woman... (1 Cor 11:12).[9]

When compared with earlier works, De Fraine's commentary is most generous in its description of the man–woman relationship. Yet it is strange that on the one hand he says that man and woman are equal, while on the other hand he says that woman must be subject to man. Basically this means: 'man and woman are equal, but he is superior and she is inferior.' In a sense, it is not too surprising that the text was understood in this way. Its author was most probably a male, since most scribes that we know of were males. Even in our society it took a long time for girls to get the same educational opportunities as boys. The interpreters of the text, until recently, were also male, often rabbis, monks, priests, ministers. A text written by a male and interpreted by a male will lead to a 'male reading.'

---

9 J. De Fraine, *The Bible and the Origin of Man* (New York: Desclée, 1962), pp. 44-45.

But things have changed; such interpretation is no longer acceptable. Thanks to the Women's Liberation Movement and to the increased number of female exegetes, this text has been reread and re-interpreted. Some have even come to the opposite conclusion that 'man and woman are equal, but she is superior and he is inferior.'

We will now examine the most significant arguments of exegetes belonging to the first group and compare them with the arguments of the second group to see who will win the battle for superiority in equality! Let it be clear that not all men are on one side of the discussion, nor are all women on the other.

a. The Man Is Created First, the Woman Last

The paradise story starts with the creation of the man (Gen 2:7). The man is, therefore, first in the mind of the creator, and everything that God makes subsequently is given to the man for his happiness. Obviously the whole story centres around the man. We might also remember the prominence given to the first-born son in biblical narratives, thus, in this case, the man.

But these arguments are now reversed. The concept of the first-born cannot be invoked here. The fact that the woman appears at the end of creation, far from implying her inferiority, proves her superiority to man. All exegetes know that, in the priestly account of creation, humankind appeared as the last work of the last day (1:26). They all agree that the whole story was built towards the creation of humankind, everything was ready to receive humankind to reign over the universe. If, in all logic, we apply the same principle here, then we must admit that the woman, who was created last in the paradise story (2:21-22), must also be the crown of God's creation.

There exist a number of mythological texts stating that God gained experience as creation progressed. This is also the case in the paradise story. God did not succeed too well creating man, gained experience creating the animals, and so was ready to create his masterpiece, the woman. The special dignity of the woman is further stressed by the fact that God took counsel only for her creation (2:18), as he did for the creation of humankind in the creation narrative (1:26). And finally, man's creation is narrated in a single verse (2:7), while the creation of woman is much more elaborate, thereby emphasizing her importance.

b. The Woman Is Taken from the Man, but the Man from the Soil

It has been stressed that the woman proceeds from the man, "Yahweh God built the rib he had taken *from the man* into a woman" (2:22). Necessarily, the whole is superior to the part.

An argument from such a position can lead to rather strange conclusions. The text says that "Yahweh God fashioned man of dust *from the soil*" (2:7). The text uses the same "from" as for the creation of the woman. If the man is superior because the woman is from the man, then the earth, from which the man is taken, must be superior to the man. Is it not a sign of greater perfection that woman is created from organic material, while the man only from inorganic matter, which he has in common with the animals also fashioned from the soil?

Some exegetes place considerable emphasis upon the different verbs used to describe the creation of each. Though Yahweh "fashioned" man (2:7), he "built" the woman (2:22). Since "built" in Hebrew connotes a reliability which is not suggested in the previous verb, the vocabulary also confirms woman's superiority.

c. The Woman Is the Helper of the Man

Yahweh puts the man in the garden to take care of it; the text clearly indicates that everything centres on the man. Having entrusted the garden to man, God wants to give him even more, "It is not good that man should be alone. I will make him a helper fit for him" (2:18). It is difficult to be any clearer: the woman is made as man's helper. In actuality, the "helper" has often even become the 'servant.'

A more precise study of the word "helper" *(ezer)* has shown that it is rarely used for a human being. Most often it refers to God. God is the helper of the needy and the desperate, "Our soul awaits Yahweh, he is our help and shield" (Ps 33:20). Yet it is impossible to consider man superior to God, the helper. The "helper" therefore does not imply that woman is inferior to man, but rather that man needs her, that he cannot live without her. Thus when the paradise story speaks of woman as man's helper, it places her in a relationship to man similar to that of God when it speaks of him as man's "helper."

d. The Woman Was Tempted First

Not only does the man know that he is superior to the woman, but the serpent also is aware of her inferiority. The history of exegesis once again provides us with a rich variety of explanations as to just why the serpent tempted the woman first (Gen 3:1). The common answer is that since woman is weaker and more curious than man, the serpent had a greater chance of success. And from there followed the long tradition of Eve the temptress, while man was almost totally innocent. "In woman was sin's beginning, and because of her we all die" (Sirach 25:23), and "Adam was not deceived, but the woman was deceived and became a transgressor" (1 Timothy 2:14).

But once the symbolism of the story is understood, the reason why the serpent starts with the woman becomes obvious. The serpent, a creature related to the cult of fertility and fecundity, speaks to the woman first because it is she who gives life. It was not an uncommon practice in some ancient Near Eastern cultures for women to visit the serpent-goddess that they might have children, but this obviously was done with the consent of their husbands. When Jeremiah accuses the women of idolatry, they answer, "when we burned incense to the queen of heaven and poured out libations to her, was it without our husband's approval that we made cakes for her bearing her image and poured out libations to her?" (Jeremiah 44:19). It is this type of approval which took place in the garden, "She gave some also to her husband *who was with her*" (Gen 3:6). The whole text seems to suggest that he was there with her, from the beginning, and did not object whatsoever.

Several exegetes are now inclined to reverse the roles. According to them, the woman seems to be the superior figure of the story. The serpent chooses her because if she eats, the man will automatically imitate her behaviour. The woman does the talking, she gives the answers, she interprets the divine commandment, she appreciates and judges, while the man simply takes the fruit and eats. She comes out as a much stronger personality, while he thinks only of his stomach. For years, many have thought of Eve as the temptress and of Adam as her poor innocent victim; now, interestingly enough, some refer to Eve as the theologian and to Adam as the brute.

Whatever one may think of the arguments on both sides, and they often both seem convincing, this example has proved very clearly that a particular predisposition of the reader affects the interpretation of a text.

4. Religious or Materialistic Reading

Brueggemann suggests in his study of the paradise story[10] that the yahwistic writer, living at the time of David–Solomon and having observed how God treated David, considers this the paradigm of how God treats any human person. Brueggemann as a believer reads the story

---

[10] See above, pp. 32-36.

from a religious point of view. The God of the paradise story is really God, the same who was active in the life of David. The man and woman of the paradise story are compared with another human being, David.

Other readers, for instance J. Guichard and J. M. Kennedy,[11] approach the text from a totally different point of view. They refuse to read the paradise story as a 'sacred' text. Rather they view it as the product of literary activity like any other narrative. They insist that any narrative is part of a historical process and, as such, is strongly influenced by the social, political and economic conditions of the time in which the text was composed. They stress that these societal structures often favour the institution and, instead of being at the service of people, end up oppressing them. Religion, because it preaches obedience to authority, is accused of favouring the *status quo* in unjust societies. Religion has, therefore, been called the "opium of the people."

The Yahwist wrote during the time of the monarchy, a period of very profound change in the social structures of Israel. Under Moses and during the first years of the conquest, the people lived as semi-nomads. In such a society all members are equal. But with the monarchy, a

---

[11] J. Guichard, "Approche 'matérialiste' du récit de la chute. Genèse 3," in *Lumière et vie*, 26 (1977), n. 131, pp. 57-90; J. M. Kennedy, "Peasants in Revolt: Political Allegory in Genesis 2-3," in *Journal for the Study of the Old Testament*, 47 (1990), pp. 3-14; also M. Millet, "Le tournant d'une société: Le royaume de Salomon (970-930 av. J.C.) (Une vision nouvelle de la foi, Le Yahviste de Genèse II)," in *Masses Ouvrières*, 397 (1985), pp. 37-46 and 399 (1985), pp. 45-60.

whole bureaucratic system appears — civil servants, scribes, professional army, police — financed by levied taxes. This new system came to its perfection under Solomon. It also gave rise to the struggle of the different classes, the rich and the poor. But in Israel the monarchy was highly regarded because of its religious character, as was the case in Western Europe much later. To ensure the obedience of the populace, the king was presented as God's representative here on earth. As God created an orderly world out of chaos, so the king created an orderly united kingdom out of the chaos of the different tribes. And as God protected the orderly world against the powers of chaos, so the king protected Israel against the powers of its enemies.

A person like the Yahwist, who knew how to write in the tenth century before Christ, must certainly have belonged to the elite, the rich, the civil service. Thus the interest of the Yahwist was not to speak about what happened to humanity in the beginning, how Adam and Eve refused to obey God. His interest was the defence and preservation of the system. The paradise story is written to solve the problem posed by tendencies to revolt among the peasantry. It is pure propaganda for the monarchy.

Yahweh God plants a beautiful garden in which he puts man. The trees of the garden offer man plenty to eat (2:8-9, 16). God really provides man with all he needs. Man, however, is not put in this paradise to enjoy life, but "to cultivate and take care of it" (2:15). All this corresponds perfectly to the structure of Israel's society at the time of Solomon. The king lives in a paradise while his subjects live in a patronage system of peasant organization. The institution, which owns the land, controls the distribution of goods and the loyal peasant performs various services in return.

The famous “tree of the knowledge of good and evil” of which God tells man, “you are not to eat, for on the day you eat of it you shall most surely die” (2:17), represents what the king refuses the peasant. Civilization, philosophy, science, art and any type of knowledge are reserved for the elite. If peasants receive education, they may become dissatisfied with their condition and attempt to undermine the system. If this happens, the king certainly has the power to make the peasants disappear: they may indeed die the day they tried. The command to not eat of the tree is given to preserve the *status quo.*

The serpent tries to convince the woman to eat of the tree, by letting her know all she is missing, “God knows in fact that on the day you eat it your eyes will be opened and you will be like gods, knowing good and evil” (3:5). The serpent represents all those in society who would make the people aware of what they are missing, who would enlighten the people on how the king wants to retain all privileges for himself, and who would try to educate the people in the hope of inciting rebellion against the oppression and changing the system.

Peasants who rebel against the system will bear the consequences. The curses of the paradise story (3:14-19) reflect the severe realities of peasant existence, the hard socio-economic conditions of rural life, "with sweat on your brow shall you eat your bread" (3:19).

But of course the king has been very generous towards these ungrateful rebel peasants. He has shown them his graciousness by not killing them! He expels them, however, from his domain (3:24). Even if these people had been living in an oppressive system, they had at least some security, but now, they have nothing left. How will they ever survive? The conclusion of the story teaches in a very clear way that the social struggle of the peasants will always be to the advantage of the elite. They have the power and thus the last word.

That this paradise story was interpreted in a very different way until now is not surprising. The text was used by exegetes, belonging to the wealthy educated classes, and often to the clergy, who made it a story of Adam and Eve and their rebellion against God. It became the story of 'original sin,' which explained suffering, oppression and hard labour. People were told that all their misery is the consequence of original sin and that nothing could ever change this, because it is God's decision. The rich and the oppressors have thus been able to justify and to keep their position. The materialistic or Marxist reader claims to have liberated the text from clerical, conservative and oppressive exegesis.

The difference between the religious reading of Brueggemann, who even suggests that the text criticizes the behaviour of the king, and the materialistic reading of Guichard and Kennedy, who see the text as pure propaganda for the king, is rather striking. In the first approach,

King David, himself human, is taken as the image of every human person. In the second approach, King David is the image of an oppressive God. Both readings are based on the presupposition that the writer of the paradise story is the Yahwist and that the Yahwist wrote during the second part of King Solomon's reign. But, as we have seen, the date of the Yahwist and even the existence of the Yahwist are now under attack, which of course puts these readings into question. Whatever the outcome of the Yahwist question and the validity of these two studies, these two types of readings show very clearly how the convictions of the reader influence his or her interpretation.

III. Advantages and Limitations of a Reader-centred Interpretation

What we have described are the approaches taken by new methods in the field of biblical studies, such as *reader-response criticism, narrative criticism, feminist interpretation,* and *Marxist or materialistic interpretation.* All these methods now favour the reader because the reader gives meaning to the text. These methods trust the reader, who dares to approach the text with much more creativity, knowing that many readings are acceptable. And since readers are so different from one another and each one evolves continually, the same text will receive many meanings. Roland Barthes wrote once, "A literary work has eternal value, not because all people discover in it the same meaning, but because it invites each reader to more than one meaning." All this is far removed from the search for *the* meaning intended by the author.

On the other hand, the preceding examples have shown that there can be not only a variety of interpretations, but even contradictory interpretations. The reasoning in the male reading may sound correct, and so may the reasoning in the female reading, but is it possible that the same text could speak of male superiority in equality between man and woman, and at the same time of female superiority in equality between the two? Is it possible to accept that the same text, when it speaks of God, means indeed God, as in the religious reading, and then that God does not mean God but the king, as in the materialistic reading, which then becomes in fact an allegorical interpretation of the text?

It is rather interesting to note this return to the allegorical interpretation of the scriptures, especially since such interpretations by the early rabbis and Fathers of the Church no longer impress most modern readers. People who have difficulty seeing in the love between man and woman in the Song of Songs an allegory of the love of God for his people are suddenly willing to accept that God in the paradise story is not God, but the king.

All our readings are subjective. It is unavoidable and, in many ways, it is good. We always read the text through what we are and through what we bring to the text. But could it be that some readings become subjectivistic? A reader may use the text to prove his or her point or theory: the text becomes a pretext. The basic distinction between what is called *exegesis* (what we bring out of the text) and *eisegesis* (what we impose upon the text when we read our own interpretation into the text) remains valid. Who or what is going to decide that this subjective reading respects the text and is good, sound exegesis, while the other reading is subjectivistic and pure eisegesis?

III

The Text Is the Judge

I. Presuppositions and Theory of a Text-centred Interpretation

The spoken and the written word are the most common means of human communication. Much of what has been said in the two preceding chapters applies equally to the spoken and to the written word. The listener or the reader tries to find out what the speaker or the writer wants to say, but the listener or the reader receives that word according to his or her predispositions. Because of these similarities between spoken and written word, people have not always sufficiently noticed that there is also a very important difference.

In oral communication, there are in a sense only two actors, the speaker and the listener, and they are normally in each other's presence. There is consequently a lot of interaction between the two. The speaker notices that the listener seems to follow or appears to have difficulties or is daydreaming. He or she can read a lot in the eyes or attitudes of the other. Questions can be asked.

In this way of communication the following reactions to what is said often occur.[1] The listener may react to what is said by, "You said such and such," to which the speaker may reply, "No, I did not. I said such and such." Another reaction may be, "You said such and such" and the reply, "Oh did I? That is not what I meant. What I meant to say was such and such." Or another reaction, "You said such and such" and the reply, "Oh yes. I did not have that in mind when I spoke, but of course what I said could mean that." Or the following reaction, "You said such and such," and the reply, "Well, not exactly. You see when I use such and such a word, it has such and such associations for me. So the statement has a lot more overtones than you suggest." Or still another reaction could be, "You said such and such" and the reply, "Yes, but I would not choose to put it that way. I was trying to express it in a way that you would find easier to grasp."

These few examples illustrate how difficult it is to communicate through words and how what the listener understands does not necessarily correspond to what the speaker has in mind. It even happens that the speaker has to accept that his or her speech was unclear and that the interpretation given by the listener is indeed what he or

---

[1] Adapted from F. Young, *The Art of Performance: Towards a Theology of Holy Scripture* (London: Darton, Longman and Todd, 1990), pp. 10-11.

she has said even if this was not what he or she intended to say.

We referred to the spoken word when two persons are in each other's presence, but one readily notices a difference with the spoken word when the two are no longer present to each other. If one speaks to a person on the telephone, one can no longer observe the reactions on the face of the other person. As a professor, I enjoy teaching a group of students because I notice their reactions. But I do not like to teach alone in front of a video camera for distance education. As the speaker, I lose contact with the listeners.

One easily realizes the great difference between oral and written communication. In the latter case, the writer and the reader are no longer in each other's presence, so no questions can be asked, no reactions can be seen, and above all a third actor has appeared, the text itself.

We know that this text was once written by a historical author. We insisted upon the importance of the author, for instance, in the case of a love letter, or for people who buy a book because it is written by their favourite author. But there are other cases, where the reader does not ask himself or herself at all who wrote the text, as for instance for some articles in newspapers. Whatever the case may be, we have noticed very clearly that, even in the most optimal conditions of written communication, we will never be able to discover fully the precise intention of the author.

The writer, after having done his or her work of writing, has lost authority over this text, which no longer can be corrected: the text is now in the hands of the reader. The writer can never avoid the possible gaps in a text; these are filled in by each reader who is always different. And as we saw, this explains why each reader gives meaning to the text. This meaning may or may not correspond to the intended meaning of the author. Just as, in oral communication, the speaker sometimes has to admit that what the listener has understood is indeed what the speaker has said, even if it is not what the speaker intended to say, in the same way, in written communication, the writer may have to admit that the text does indeed say what the reader has perceived, even if the writer did not have that in mind. In law, judges interpret the text of the law and not what the legislator intended; the only thing they work with is the law.

We could even say that there are cases where reading the text according to the meaning of the historical writer would lead to unfaithfulness to the text. The following example may illustrate this. In Washington, the capital of the United States, close by the White House and the Capitol, a monument commemorates president Jefferson. On its walls are different impressive texts of this important American leader. One of them states: "We hold these truths to be self-evident: that all men are created equal," which is a very clear statement about the fundamental equality of all human beings. This text actually became part of the American Declaration of Independence. We know that in Jefferson's day there were still slaves, so the question arises, What was the meaning of this text at that time? The leaders of the American colonies realized that in their fight for independence they had the right to demand self-determination from England. What people then did not see was that they did not apply that same principle in favour of their black slaves. Blacks, in their eyes, were not fully human. In a very real sense, when the leaders spoke of "all men," they meant only 'adult white males.' This text today is understood very differently because society has advanced a long way in the fight for equal rights for all persons. But could a fervent animal lover quote Jefferson's statement to request the same rights for animals as for humans? Of course not. In other words, there seem to be limits on the freedom of interpretations given by the reader.

This illustrates very clearly that a written text is a reality unto itself. In the final analysis, the text will be the last judge of which meanings are acceptable and which unacceptable. An author-centred interpretation investigates the world *behind* the text, a reader-centred interpretation favours the world *in front of* the text, a text-centred interpretation focuses on the world *within* the text.

Much research has gone into discovering the world which created the book, but the world within the text has been somewhat neglected. A text is a world of its own. Some texts may even become independent of the prevailing historical, social, economic and political conditions. Their value and meaning transcend these changing factors and seem to have a kind of 'eternal' value. The limited, restricted, finite world of the author is replaced by the unlimited, unrestricted, infinite world of the text. This certainly applies to the Bible, which is not limited to one culture.

A text is a network of relations and structures, beautifully held together, which give it unity. Thus it is obvious that the text-centred interpretation opts for a *synchronic* approach to texts. It takes the text as it is *now,* in its final form and, for the biblical text, we can add in its canonical form. The canon of the Bible, the collection of books considered normative, contains the books in their definitive form.

This text-centred interpretation is thus very different from the author-centred interpretation which is *diachronic* and examines the growth of the text, searching for the different layers of the text through source criticism or through redaction criticism. The diachronic approach studies the text in its historical development and looks in a sense for the pre-text, for what precedes the final text, often with the implication that what was at the beginning is the real thing and that the subsequent elements corrupted the original meaning. It may be very true that the text has a long history, but the so-called irregularities or lack of logic of that text, which suggest to some the existence of different layers, are often more in the mind of the reader than in the text itself. The reader who takes the text as it is has to struggle with the text and may discover its beautiful unity. The growth of the original text can be seen as something very positive and even teach us what reading is: constant growth and new actualization.

If texts can be read by people who perhaps do not even know the writer, who may belong to a totally different cultures and different periods in time, there must be something in texts that makes reading them possible. This something is found in the threefold relations of the text. There are, first of all, the relations within the text itself, *intra-textual relations*; words relate to other words, sentences to other sentences. Secondly, a text is related to other texts, *inter-textual relations*,[2] which of course will help the reader to understand a new text he or she reads. Finally a text is related to reality, *extra-textual relations*; for instance, the reader will understand the word 'table' in a text because he or she knows what a table is in the real world. We will now concentrate on the intra-textual relations.[3]

The basic principle is that *any discourse respects a grammar*. A discourse, which is a text longer than a sentence, is kept together through structures, through a set of laws which makes the text a network of operations and relations. Everything in the text, even if some elements may be called later additions, is important and keeps the whole together. The comparison with the sentence has led to this conclusion. If a sentence has a grammar, each discourse must also have a grammar.

---

[2] E. van Wolde, "Van tekst via tekst naar betekenis: Intertekstualiteit en haar implicaties," in *Tijdschrift voor theologie*, 30 (1990), pp. 333-61.

[3] W. Vogels, *Reading & Preaching the Bible: A New Semiotic Approach* (*Background Books,* 4) (Wilmington, Delaware: Michael Glazier, Inc., 1986).

Let us start from the following sentence as an example: "Johnny loves Betty." In this sentence we can distinguish three levels. The first level is what appears at the surface, what any reader sees. We notice two proper names, we also notice that they both end with 'y,' giving the sentence a poetic character; we could even speak of assonance. This is the level of what we could call the *style*.

The second level is hidden and is no longer visible on the surface. 'Johnny' in this sentence is the subject, 'loves' is the verb, and 'Betty' is the object. We now have reached the level of *syntax*. We have discovered the structure that any sentence has to respect to be understandable: subject, verb, object. A child learning to speak might say "Milk likes I," and would be corrected by the parents to say "I like milk." Thus, we start applying that grammatical rule spontaneously even as children. Only later, when we study grammar, do we realize what we have been doing all along and what we continue to do unconsciously. We don't stop to ask ourselves, before formulating our next sentence, who or what the subject will be and who or what the object will be. It all falls into place automatically because it corresponds to something within us. Knowing this rule, we can now analyse any sentence. 'Johnny' can be replaced by 'I,' 'she' or whatever, the verb 'loves' by 'drink,' or 'writes,' and the object 'Betty' by 'coffee' or 'a letter' (e.g. "I drink coffee" or "She writes a letter"). This rule is valid not only for all sentences in English but for all languages. It is a universal rule. This explains why people of different languages and cultures can communicate with each other and also why translations are possible, even of texts which were written centuries ago. The discovered rule transcends cultural and historical differences and corresponds to a universal human structure. One can already foresee the important consequences if there were something similar in any literary text longer than a sentence, if every text followed some basic universal rule.

We have discovered that Johnny is the subject, which means that *he* loves Betty, and we have understood something important in that sentence. But the sentence does not say if Betty loves Johnny too. Still, the reader will ask other questions about that sentence, like Who is Johnny? Who is Betty? What type of love is implied? We have now reached the third level, which also is hidden and does not appear on the surface. It is the level of the thematic values, of *semantics*. Johnny can be Betty's father, he can be her husband or her neighbour; maybe Betty is Johnny's cat! And of course these different possibilities affect the meaning.

We have thus noticed that in this sentence the two actors, Johnny and Betty, play two types of roles. Johnny plays the narrative role of subject and the thematic role of, for instance, loving husband. Betty too plays two roles, the narrative role of object and the thematic role of beloved spouse.

What we have said about the three levels of a simple sentence can help to understand the three levels of any literary unit longer than a sentence. The first level is also the surface of the text where we notice structures, *surface structures*. People have studied these types of structures for many years, in many areas including biblical studies. We speak of the introduction, the body and the conclusion of a text, we notice repetitions of key words, refrains; we speak of parallel structures (A-B-C / A'-B'-C') or of chiastic structures (A-B-C / C'-B'-A').[4] All this remains at the surface level of the text.

The second level, which in the sentence corresponds to the syntax, is hidden and analyses the narrative movement of the text. The text moves by virtue of the *narrative structures* which follow their own narrative grammar, a set of laws governing the organization of the narrativity.

The third level, which in the sentence corresponds to the semantics, is also hidden and analyses the thematic values of the text. Because any text is a type of discourse, they are called the *discursive structures,* a set of laws governing the semantic organization of the text.

The comparison with the sentence also shows that we are here touching universal human structures common to all cultures and to all types of literature. Scholars have discovered these structures and have made us aware of what we were doing unconsciously as we wrote, like after we studied the syntax of the sentence and realized what we had been doing since our early childhood. A writer of a text has great freedom, but he or she always respects the grammar of a text, otherwise the text would become meaningless. And because the reader also is human and

---

4 See example, p. 98.

thus works with the same structures, communication is possible through a text because he or she can discover what is happening in the text. He or she can discover the world within the text. And because all meaningful texts are held together by these structures, all texts can be understood by the reader. Translations are possible, old texts can still be appreciated.

We could compare with a game of chess where two players are at work. The two may not know each other at all, may belong to different cultures, but they can play because both respect the rules of the game. And still, each game is so different because each player has nearly an infinite number of ways in which he or she may move the pieces. The rules make it possible for people to play the game while freedom makes it possible for each individual game to be exciting.

All texts are different and that is why reading is so exciting. At the same time, reading is only possible because all texts respect the universal common structures. The knowledge of these structures provides the reader with the key to unlock each text and also to discover where the text will be open to, or resist, meanings. Therefore, the text will play the role of judge in the numerous meanings that readers give to the same text.

1. The Narrative Structures

In a text, only two things can be said about a person. A person 'is' — he or she is in a particular state (rich, happy, sick, asleep, etc.) — or a person 'does' — he or she acts. To make a story move, a verb of the type 'to do' is needed, and this action will change the state of the person. A story is thus constituted by a begin-state, a transformation and an end-state.

If everything were already in place, there would be no story. If Adam and Eve were already there, the story could not tell of their appearance on earth. The *begin-state* is, therefore, always a negative state, not negative in a moral sense, but simply in the sense that something is lacking, something is not yet there. If the transformation succeeds, then of course the lack will have disappeared and the end-state will be a positive state.

The *transformation* moves through different steps. The first step is called the *manipulation*. This word does not have the pejorative connotations it has in daily usage, but is a technical term which wants to include all possibilities to say that someone, the sender, will push a subject to act to overcome the perceived lack. The sender can decide to do it him- or herself, and thus become also the subject, or the sender can assign someone else to do the job. And of course this can take many different forms. The sender can order, invite, provoke, tempt, or whatever, the subject to act. In the paradise story, God, the sender, decides to create Adam and Eve, and he decides to do it himself, and thus to become the subject.

The second step of the transformation is the *competence*. The subject cannot respond to the manipulation of the sender if he or she (the subject) is not competent. This competence presupposes three things: the subject must have the *will* to act, the *ability* to act and the *knowledge* to act. The acquisition of this competence by the subject may be a long process in the story. It may well be that the subject needs helpers or has to overcome opponents. Many transformations never succeed because the subject did not reach the necessary competence. In the gospel, there are reports that Jesus could not perform any miracles at a particular place because of the lack of faith of the people.

3. Once the competence is acquired, the story can move to the third step, the *performance*, in which the subject does the action which will bring about the transformation from the begin-state to the end-state.

4. And finally, there is often a fourth step in the story, the *sanction*. Someone evaluates the preceding performance to decide if it is well done or if something is still missing. This evaluation consists in a recognition and is often accompanied by a retribution. Once more, these terms, sanction and retribution, must not be understood in a punitive sense.

If all this has worked, then the story will have reached the *end-state*, in which the lack from the beginning has disappeared. It is the positive state, but note once more that this has no moral connotations.

These are the basic narrative structures of texts. Each step requires the other and when one step is accomplished, the text can move on, but only in the order and succession we have indicated. The performance can never happen if the subject has not first acquired the competence, and nobody acts unless he or she is somehow motivated to do so. No evaluation can happen unless the action has been done. It may however be that in a text some steps are not explicitly mentioned, but they are there implicitly. It may well be that, after the manipulation, the text moves to the performance without describing the competence. But the reader can fill that gap, because he or she knows for certain that only a competent subject can act.

The following diagram summarizes the narrative sequence of a text:

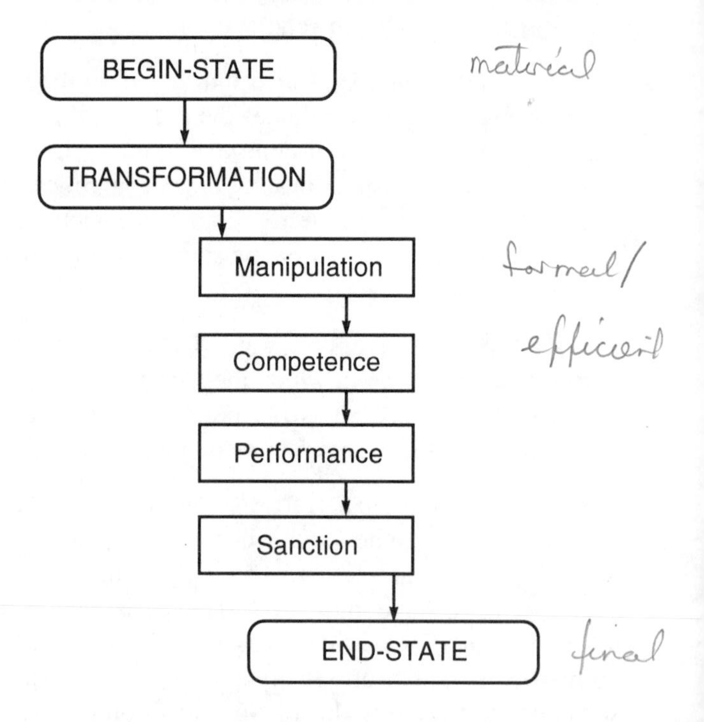

2. The Discursive Structures

The narrative analysis has uncovered the operations in the text, the succession of everything that happens in the text. Clearly it helps to find out what is the story's real lack which has been transformed, in other words what the story is all about. It helps also to see exactly who does what. We did compare this part of the reading with the study of the syntax in the analysis of a sentence, which also clearly states who the subject is. But there is much more to a text than the narrative structures and, as we do in the sentence, we also look for the semantic values of the text, the relationships between the different themes in the text.

Each actor in the story plays an actantial role as, for instance, sender, subject or helper, as well as a thematic role. The subject may be a woman, she may be a widow, she may be sick, and thus the *themes* of the text are important. The analysis has to discover which themes are selected in the text.

The human mind follows a binary logic. A word has meaning through, and because of, difference. We could not speak of rich people if there were no poor people; when we hear high, we also hear low, young – old, man – woman, parent – child. Only these themes in which we discover *oppositions* are important, because a text is precisely a transformation from one state to another.

But in the forest of all possible multiple themes and their opposites, there is something which must hold the whole text together and give *coherence* to the text. The reader always begins his or her reading with the many semantic values that appear in the text, classifies them in opposite pairs and, by reducing them more and more, hopes eventually to reach one or two fundamental oppositions which give coherence to the whole text. The reader goes in the opposite direction from the writer who proceeds from a fundamental idea which he or she wants to communicate and develops it in increasing detail.

Each element of a text receives its actual meaning through its relation to the other elements and through its opposite term. A text is a game of relationships. Indeed, we could speak of a network in which everything is linked together in relationship and in which each element is, therefore, essential. If an element is mentioned in a text, it has a function at both the narrative and the discursive levels. The text is like a sweater: by pulling one strand of yarn, one can unravel the entire garment.

The narrative analysis has uncovered the narrative structures, in other words the operations in the text. The discursive analysis has classified the semantic values with their opposites and has thus uncovered the discursive structures, in other words the relationships within the text. The two have now to be brought together. The narrativity will indicate in what direction the themes are moved in the story.

II. A Text-centred Interpretation of Genesis 2–3

The reader who uses a text-centred analysis for the paradise story takes the text as it stands now with all its elements and searches for the narrative and the discursive structures.[5]

1. The Narrative Structures

The text starts with, "At the time when... there was as yet no wild bush on the earth nor had any wild plant yet sprung up" (Gen 2:5). The *begin-state* is clearly a negative state. Something is missing. The earth is like a desert, devoid of vegetation. The reason for this lack is double. First, there is no rain, "for Yahweh God had not sent rain on the earth" (2:5) and, second, there is no farmer, "nor was there any *adam* to till the soil" (2:5).

Here arises a difficulty in the analysis. Readers are generally inclined to translate *adam* by "man," thinking of a male, because the woman appears later in the story. But the reader does not know that yet, he or she has not reached that part of the narrative and does not possess that information. The first place to search for the actual meaning of the word *adam* is the sentence in which the

[5] W. Vogels, "L'être humain appartient au sol. Gen 2,4b-3,24," in *Nouvelle revue théologique*, 105 (1983), pp. 515-34; W. Vogels, *Reading & Preaching the Bible: A New Semiotic Approach* (*Background Books*, 4) (Wilmington, Delaware: Michael Glazier, Inc., 1986), pp. 106-29. For a different synchronic study of the same text, R. Hinschberger, "Une lecture synchronique de Gen 2-3," in *Revue des sciences religieuses*, 63 (1989), pp. 1-16.

word is used. The sentence speaks about the cultivation of the soil, which is done not only by males, but also by females. In some cultures, the females do even more cultivating than the males. Furthermore, the person who has just finished reading the preceding creation narrative has already encountered the same term *adam*, "God created *adam*... male and female he created them" (1:27). In this verse, the word clearly refers to the human being in general, who is then identified as male and female. There are, therefore, strong reasons taken from the text itself to suggest that the word *adam* at the beginning of the paradise story refers to a human being in general, without necessarily implying that it is a male. Therefore, the text says, "nor was there any human being to till the soil" (2:5).

The reason for the lack of vegetation is double: there is no rain and there is nobody to cultivate the soil. But the text goes on, "However, a flood was rising from the earth..." (2:6). The first reason for this lack is about to be overcome. Even if there is no rain, there is some type of subterranean water coming to the surface. Such water could produce a result similar to rain, if there were a human being to channel this flood. This would make vegetation possible. So the only real lack left is that there is no human being yet.

The logic of the narrative moves therefore into the creation of a human being, "Yahweh God fashioned the human being of dust from the soil..." (2:7). The text mentions directly the *performance* of which Yahweh is the subject. Since Yahweh takes the decision and seems to be his own sender, we could speak of *automanipulation*, and God obviously has the *competence* to carry out the action, as his performance shows. This newly created human being is closely linked with the soil, because he is fashioned from the soil.

In a sense, because the two lacks have disappeared, the story is over, but we know that the paradise story will go on. It looks, therefore, as though we have reached the end of what we could call a micro-text (2:4b-7), which has presented the relationship between the human being and the earth (this is even clearer in Hebrew because of the similarity between the words *adam* [human being] and *adamah* [soil, earth]). If a new story were to follow, the normal sequence that the reader would expect would be a story of how this newly created human being starts cultivating the soil since that is the reason for the human's creation. The human being could make the desert bloom.

The text, however, moves in an unexpected direction. To the surprise of the reader, the text says that it is not this human being but God who becomes the farmer, "Yahweh God planted a garden in Eden which is in the east, and there he put the human being he had fashioned" (2:8-9). The text describes two *performances* by the same competent subject, Yahweh God. The text says how beautiful the garden is with plenty of water (2:10-14), contrary to the desert at the beginning.

Yahweh God, who has been until now the subject of several performances, becomes the sender of the human being, who is now put into the position of subject. The text moves into a *manipulation* (2:15-17). There are positive commands, 'having to do.' The human being is placed in the garden "to cultivate and take care of it" (2:15) and "may eat indeed of all the trees in the garden" (2:16). But there is also a prohibition, 'having not to do,' "Nevertheless of the tree of the knowledge of good and evil you are not to eat…," and the *sanction* is added, "for on the day you eat of it you shall most surely die" (2:17). Until now, the text confirms that *adam* refers to a human being, that is, man and woman could eat of these trees and not eat of that one tree; otherwise, the rest of the story becomes difficult to understand. If the prohibition were only for Adam, then Eve could have eaten from that tree.

The reader now would expect to find a description of how the human being starts to cultivate the divine garden or of his eating or not eating of the fruits of the trees. Instead of such performances by the human being, the text presents Yahweh God reflecting (2:18). We have to conclude once more that another micro-text (2:8-17), which concentrated on the manipulation without telling what happened, has come to an end. This micro-text speaks about the relationship between God and the human being. The human person is accepted into God's garden, but has no access to the centre of the garden. The relationship between God and the human being is one of closeness and of distance. God remains God, the human being has to remain human.

So instead of telling about a possible performance by the human being, the text goes on to say, "Yahweh God said, 'It is not good that the human being should be alone.

I will make him a helpmate'" (2:18). Now, if the paradise story is one literary unit, then all these micro-texts must have some connection to each other. Yahweh's statement clearly refers to something which happened before. The verse contains a *sanction*, a negative evaluation, a disapproval. Yahweh evaluates his own performance from the first micro-text. He had created a human being to cultivate the soil, but now he admits that what he did then "is not good." This statement indicates not only a disapproval, but also a lack. We are thus again in the *begin-state* of a new story.

It is not good for a human being to be alone. This is true for man, but equally true for woman. This proves once again that until now the text is speaking about the human person in general. The text also indicates that Yahweh is once more his own sender through *automanipulation*, "I will make." Apparently he also has all the necessary competence, because he moves as subject directly into the *performance*, "So from the soil Yahweh God fashioned all the wild beasts..." (2:19). This performance is followed by a *sanction* by the human person for whom Yahweh God had wanted to create a helpmate. The human person evaluates these animals, gives them names, "but no helpmate suitable for a human being was found for him" (2:20). The recognition is clearly a disapproval.

Yahweh could have left it at that, but he accepts the disapproval and wants to correct it. He moves into a second *performance*. He takes a rib of this human being and now two new beings are in each other's presence.

Out of one creature two appear: a human being with one rib less, and a human being formed from this rib. The story now for the first time uses the words 'man' *(ish)* and 'woman' *(ishah)* (2:23). A new *sanction* follows this second performance, "This at last..." (2:23). This time the recognition is a positive approval. The second performance has been a success.

The text concludes, "This is why a man leaves his father and mother and joins himself to his wife, and they become one body" (2:24). The lack in the begin-state has been overcome after a transformation through two performances, the first unsuccessful and the second successful. The *begin-state* is described as, "It is not good... to be alone" (2:18) and in the *end-state* the two "become one body" (2:24). Has anything really changed? What was one in the beginning is still (or again) one at the end. But something has changed indeed: the oneness of the beginning, which was loneliness, has become the oneness of relationship.

Another micro-text (2:18-24) has come to an end. It described the relationship between a human person and the animals, and the relationship between man and woman.

But the whole paradise story is not over yet. The text continues, "Now both of them were naked, the man and his wife, but they felt no shame in front of each other" (2:25). We are in the *begin-state* of a new story. There is a lack: they are naked, which structurally is opposed to being clothed. Man and woman are there now in each other's presence in all their nakedness, conscious of their limitations. They know that they are not God, as indicated in the second micro-text (2:8-17), but also that, as man or as woman, they are only half of humankind, as shown in the third micro-text (2:18-24). But, says the text, they "felt no shame." The lack in the story, structurally speaking, does not correspond to a psychological lack. They can live happily with what they are.

The story will move on only if someone can convince them to feel unhappy about these limitations. The serpent, "the most subtle of all the wild beasts that Yahweh God had made" (3:1), will play this role. The link is made with the preceding micro-text: the human being had given names to the animals, showing his power over them (2:20), and now an animal wants to overpower the human being.

The dialogue between the serpent and the woman is a typical case of *manipulation* to create the 'will to act.' The woman finds herself in a conflict situation. There are now *two* senders. God has given the command not to eat and the woman is in the position of 'having not to eat,' with death as the sanction. But the serpent tempts and invites the woman to eat; it tries to put the woman in the position of 'wanting to eat,' with, as *sanction*, the statement that she will not die but will become divine (3:4-5). Finally man and woman follow the invitation of the serpent and move into the *performance:* they eat of the forbidden tree (3:6).

After the performance follows the *sanction*. The serpent had promised, "on the day you eat it your eyes will be opened and you will be like gods knowing good and evil" (3:5). And indeed it seems to have worked, "Then the eyes of both of them were opened...," but they see something very different from what the serpent had promised them, "...they realized that they were naked" (3:7). The performance did not succeed. Instead of finding themselves without limitations, they see now, more clearly than ever, how limited they are.

Their nakedness, which formerly was not felt as a lack, becomes now a painful discovery, and "so they sewed fig-leaves together to make themselves loincloths" (3:7). From accepting their limitations without any shame in front of each other, they end up being ashamed and hide behind their clothes. The *end-state* of another micro-text (2:25–3:7) has been reached; it describes the disturbed relationship between animal and human being, and between man and woman.

The story could be over, but God intervenes and a new text starts. The beginning refers again to the nakedness. God calls the man to find where he is hiding and the man answers, "I was naked, so I hid" (3:10). The human being, who has just clothed himself, recognizes himself to be naked in front of God. They may hide their limitations in front of each other, but in front of God they are still there in all their nakedness.

What follows in the paradise story is the *sanction* by God who had put the human being in the position of 'having not to do.' What has been the performance of the subject? First comes the recognition. God wants to verify the truth of what has happened, "Have you been eating of the tree I forbade you to eat…" (3:11-13). Then follows the negative retribution, with the punishment of the different actors (3:14-19).

They could hide their nakedness in front of each other, but only God can cover the profound nakedness of the human being, "Yahweh God made garments out of skins for the man and his wife and he clothed them" (3:21). The fear the human being had in front of God in the beginning (3:10) is replaced by confidence. Another micro-text is over (3:8-21); it spoke about a different relationship between God and human being.

The whole paradise story is not over yet. A final micro-text again involves a transformation from one state to another. Humanity is still in paradise, but what was announced in the punishment (3:17-19) is now happening, "So Yahweh God expelled him from the garden of Eden to till the soil from which he had been taken" (3:23). God moves the human being from the garden and returns him to the soil with the mission to till the soil, a mission for which he was created in the first place. But this soil will now resist the human person, "it shall yield you brambles and thistles" (3:18). Thus, this last micro-text (3:22-24) speaks of the broken relationship between the human person and the earth.

The end of the paradise story sends the reader back to its beginning, to the soil. The macro-text of the paradise story, in which we have discovered six micro-texts, is over.

We can summarize the story in the following schema:

A Human being and earth (2:4b-7)

B Human being and God (2:8-17)

C Human being and animals/ man and woman (2:18-24)

C' Animal vs human being/ man vs woman (2:25-3:7)

B' God vs human being (3:8-21)

A' Earth vs human being (3:22-4)

The study of the narrative structures of the text has also uncovered a chiastic structure at the surface of the text. The whole story is a diptych with two panels perfectly corresponding to each other. A-B-C speak of harmony, a world of which we dream, while C'-B'-A' speak of disharmony, the real world in which we live. The turning point is in 2:25, the acceptance or not of our limitations.

2. The Discursive Structures

We discovered the operations of the paradise story, but that same story is also a network of relationships. We will now briefly show the play of some of the thematic oppositions which hold the story together.

The oppositions in the paradise story are not only numerous, but very striking: inside paradise–outside paradise; God–human being; human being–animal; man–woman; solitude–relationship; mutual help–opposition;

good–evil; knowledge–ignorance; life–death; joy–suffering; work–toil; everything–nothing; naked–clothed; acceptance of limitations–shame; openness–hiddenness. Many more could be suggested, but these seem to be the more important ones. It becomes rather easy to see which ones are the positive and which ones the negative. People long for the positive and try to avoid the negative. We strive for the values which were in paradise.

The narrative structure of the story has shown how the acceptance or the refusal of the limitations is the turning point of the change in the thematic values (2:25). We could then summarize the whole story as follows:

- The story starts with the acceptance of what one is, limitations included. This is happiness; let us call this *peace* or paradise.
- The text then moves to the introduction of doubt; one now finds it difficult to accept these limitations. This is *temptation*.
- From there the text moves to the refusal of these limitations which leads to unhappiness. This is *sin*.

It is perhaps interesting to notice how, in this text-centred interpretation, the conflict about the superiority in the equality between man and woman has totally disappeared. The text speaks about relationships. The beginning of the text speaks about a human being, what we have in common as man and woman. And, indeed, before an animal one recognizes oneself as human and not as man or woman. The text can only speak of a man when the woman appears (2:23) and, indeed, we recognize ourselves as man or as woman in the presence of the other human being.

III. Advantages and Limitations of a Text-centred Interpretation

There are several new methods in biblical studies which are all text-centred. The method which looks at the structures at the surface of the text, the visible and more stylistic structures, is called *rhetorical criticism,* sometimes also called *literary criticism.*[6] The method which looks at the hidden structures, the narrative and discursive structures, used to be called *structural analysis,* but scholars now prefer to call it *semiotics* (the science of the signs). All these text-centred interpretations share an intention to take the text very seriously. The reader has the text and nothing else. A. J. Greimas, a well known semiotician, used to say often, "No salvation outside of the text."

The advantages of these synchronic methods are rather obvious. First of all, the text is taken in its present form and, secondly, the methods claim to touch upon universally valid rules. We all accept that once a person knows the syntax of sentences, he or she can analyse all sentences. Similarly, once the reader has understood the

[6] An example of such a study of the paradise story: J. T. Walsh, "Genesis 2:4b–3:24: A Synchronic Approach," in *Journal of Biblical Literature,* 96 (1977), pp. 161-77.

narrative and discursive structures of texts, he or she is capable of analysing all texts. And, most important, the person can do it him- or herself. This is a great step forward in biblical studies. The author-centred methods studying the world behind the text have become so complex that people often are afraid to approach the text personally and become so dependent upon the work of the experts that they sometimes read the commentaries more than the biblical text itself.

On the other hand, text-centred approaches may seem, or could become, very fundamentalist. The paradise story provides a good example of this. A person could apply all the principles of semiotics upon the story, taking it as a historical report on what Adam and Eve did historically in a paradise located in Eden, without taking into account that the story is a myth. That reader could also speak of Adam and Eve's 'sexual disorders,' not taking into account the meaning of the word "nakedness." In other words, many of the results of the author-centred interpretations are presupposed.

But by looking at the issue more carefully, we see that questions about literary genre and the meaning of words are all related to the text itself and could therefore really be said to be part of a text-centred interpretation and not only of an author-centred one. A careful analysis of the text itself would indicate to the reader that the word "nakedness" refers to human limitations and not to sexual matters. Otherwise, how could the text still say that man and woman felt naked in front of Yahweh even when they were clothed?

Conclusion

The interpretation of the Scriptures during the first two millennia has a long history. It is not an invention of modern times to use a method to read the Bible. The writers of the New Testament already had their particular way of interpreting the texts of the Old Testament. Jewish scholars had their own techniques. The Fathers of the Church followed basically two approaches, the allegorical reading, practised especially in Alexandria, and the literal, practised more in Antioch. But all these readings were always spiritual and religious.

In the 17th and 18th centuries, important changes came in the wake of the Enlightenment which stressed the importance of reason and history. Thus in the 19th century, often called "the century of history," the Bible came to be considered a historical document which had to be studied with the same methods as any other ancient text. Gradually, the historical critical method became *the* undisputed method for any serious work in biblical studies.

But in the late 1960s and early 1970s, this method came under attack. Scholars spoke of a crisis in biblical studies; some spoke of the bankruptcy or the end of the method; others bade it formal farewell. New methods started appearing in the scholarly world, often opposed by the historical critics who claimed they were unscientific. But, eventually, the pressure became so strong that these new methods also became part of the scientific biblical scene. These methods, in contrast with the historical critical methods which stressed the importance of the intention of the author, are more reader-centred or text-centred.

What then can we foresee for the third millennium? In which direction will biblical studies go? We have come to the conclusion that, in the author-centred interpretation, we will never fully discover the intention of the historical author. We still can speak of the author, but the 'real' author has become the 'implied' author, the one that the reader constructs from the text itself: what we know of the author is what he or she decides to reveal through the text. What we have to retain from this approach is the search of the world behind the text, insofar as it is possible. Scholars will have to continue this research and bring it to the ordinary Bible reader by ever better translations, trying to transpose biblical culture into our culture. In some ways, we foresee that this type of studies will diminish. Since so much historical information has been gathered during the last two centuries, it does not seem probable that many new important discoveries will be made. But one never knows! People also doubt the value of the often purely hypothetical reconstructions of the diachronic approaches to texts.

The reader-centred interpretations will always continue because, whether we like to admit it or not, every reading, including every reading of the Bible, is always subjective. This is important because such methods have a deep desire to make the Bible come alive by bringing the world in front of the text to the text. In some ways, these methods seek a more existential and thus, for believers, a more religious reading of the text. These readings give more freedom and creativity to the reader and they involve the Bible in the daily life of the reader.

But, without something to control them, these reader-centred approaches risk falling into subjectivism and ending up with the wildest readings. There was a time when condemnations by Bible commissions or other authorities tried to control the readings, but people today are reluctant to submit to this type of intervention. And still, something must control our readings. This is what the text-centred interpretations hope to offer. Such methods believe very strongly that the reader gives the meaning to the text, but that the text itself will be the final judge of whether to accept or to reject certain readings.

Selected Bibliography

Croatto, J. S. *Biblical Hermeneutics: Toward a Theory of Reading as the Production of Meaning*. Maryknoll, NY: Orbis Books, 1987.

Eco, U. *The Role of the Reader: Explorations in the Semiotics of Texts*. Bloomington: Indiana University Press, 1979.

Hayes, J. H. and C.R. Holladay. *Biblical Exegesis: A Beginner's Handbook*. Atlanta: John Knox Press, 1982.

McKnight, E. V. *Post-Modern Use of the Bible: The Emergence of Reader-Oriented Criticism*. Nashville: Abingdon Press, 1988.

Morgan, R. and J. Barton. *Biblical Interpretation (Oxford Bible Series)*. Oxford: Oxford University Press, 1988.

Ricoeur, P. "The World of the Text and the World of the Reader," in *Time and Narrative,* III. Chicago: Chicago University Press, 1988, pp. 157-79.

Ryken, L. *Words of Delight: A Literary Introduction to the Bible*. Grand Rapids, Michigan: Baker Book House, 1987.

Tate, W. R. *Biblical Interpretation: An Integrated Approach*. Peabody, Massachusetts: Hendrickson Publishers, 1991.

Vogels, W. *Reading & Preaching the Bible: A New Semiotic Approach* (*Background Books,* 4). Wilmington, Delaware: Michael Glazier, Inc., 1986.

Young, F. *The Art of Performance: Towards a Theology of Holy Scripture.* London: Darton, Longman and Todd, 1990.

NOVALIS THEOLOGICAL SERIES

AIDS and Faith

Normand Bonneau, Barbara Bozak,
André Guindon, Richard Hardy

ISBN: 2-89088-612-3
Novalis No.: 453 8001

AIDS and Faith is a resource to help pastoral and health care professionals understand what it is like to be a Christian living with AIDS. The authors reflect on the mystery of God (Bonneau); suffering and prayer (Bozak); elements of spirituality for people living with AIDS (Hardy); and

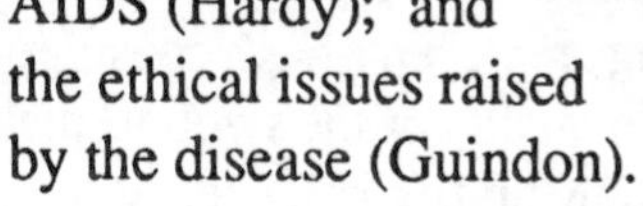
the ethical issues raised by the disease (Guindon).

NOVALIS THEOLOGICAL SERIES

Moral Development, Ethics and Faith

André Guindon

ISBN: 2-89088-533-X
Novalis No.: 497 2701

How are faith and moral development related? How does one affect the other? **Moral Development, Ethics and Faith** examines these questions in a fascinating and thoroughly original way.

Following an overview of current theories and research on stages of moral development, Dr. André Guindon examines a number of major western ethical models and shows how they reflect a specific stage of moral development. Guindon argues that the form of moral existence that each stage represents has a considerable impact on the choice and quality of the symbols that each one uses to relate to God. Moral experience, as such, does not generate faith. But when faith is present, moral experience does condition its human quality.

NOVALIS INNER JOURNEY SERIES

Spirituality has to do with our way of being religious,
with the way we experience God and with the way this
experience of God shapes our lives.

Yet not everyone knows God in the same way.
When it comes to human and Christian existence,
we all have something to learn from each other.
How do people living with AIDS experience the Lord's presence,
and what do they have to say to others? And how about
the Desert Fathers, the terminally ill, Saint Francis of Assisi and
liturgists, among others — what do they have to teach us about
relating to our deepest selves, to others and to God?

This series presents the spiritual journeys of many kinds of people.
By giving us an insider's look at the way others live their lives,
the **Novalis Inner Journey Series** helps us reflect on our
own way of being religious.

Series titles include:

IN PRINT

A Short Span of Days.

Meditation and Care for the Dying Patient,
Family and Care-giver

Laurence Freeman, O.S.B.

ISBN: 2-89088-496-1

Novalis No.: 517 5707

COMING SOON!

Healing the Heart:
Desert Wisdom for a Busy World
Kenneth C. Russell
ISBN: 2-89088-618-2

A Pillar of Fire Before Us:
Developing Liturgical Spirituality
Bernadette Gasslein
and John Hibbard
ISBN: 2-89088-576-3

Brother Fire, Sister Earth:
The Way of Saint Francis for a
Socially Responsible World
Adela Torchia
ISBN: 2-89088-617-4

Knowing the God of Compassion:
Spirituality and Persons
Living with AIDS
Richard Hardy
ISBN: 2-89088-632-8